POSITIVE AGING
A *to* Z

POSITIVE AGING
A *to* Z

TRUE STORIES
OF 26 PEOPLE
WHO TAUGHT ME
TO MAKE MY WRINKLES COUNT
INSTEAD OF
COUNTING MY WRINKLES

KAY DRIKEY
Author /Artist

Vision Books International
Santa Rosa, California

Cover Art By Linda Bushke

Vision Books International
3360 Coffey Lane, Santa Rosa, CA 95403
707-542-1440   800-377-3431   Fax 707-542-1004

Printed in the United States of America
99 98 97 96 95   6 5 4 3 2 1

Library of Congress Catalog Card Number pending

ISBN 1–56550–038–5

Table of Contents

Acknowledgments vii

Preface viii

The Aging Party xi

1. A = ADVENTURE .... *Doris Hauser* 1
   You Can't Give Love Away...It Comes Back Tomorrow

2. B = BLOOM .... *Luella Wood* 7
   Small In Stature, Large In Courage

3. C = COMMUNICATE .... *Dorothy Loa Bruegger* 12
   Turning Retire-ment Into Living-ment

4. D = DARE .... *Nina Rust* 18
   Still Cruising At 109

5. E = ENJOY .... *Edith "Edie" Morrison* 23
   Dancing Through Life

6. F = FRIENDSHIP..................... *Sumner "Pax" Paxson* 29
   Accentuate The Positive

7. G = GIVE .... *Anna Stern* 35
   Today's Elders Are Yesterday's Kids

8. H = HELP....................................... *Leonore Hollander* 41
   Can I Help?

9. I = INTERESTED & INTERESTING ... *Melba Garrett* 48
   A Rich And Wonderful Life

10. J = JAM .... *Helen King* 54
    Sing Along With Helen

11. K = KEEP FIT .... *Albert Corpening* 60
    Healthy In Body, Mind And Spirit

12. L = LEARN.................................... *Bertha Klein* 65
    Never Too Late To Learn

Contents

13. M = MENTALLY ALERT ....Hans Frey 72
    Inspired By Monet

14. N = NEVER TOO OLD ....Goldie Barclay 79
    A Century Of Living

15. O = OVERCOME ....Mary Hartzog 88
    Giving As Well As Receiving

16. P = PLAY ....Myrle Cooper 94
    The Prime Year: The Big "80"

17. Q = QUALITY ....Howard Coleman 99
    Not Enough Hours In A Day

18. R = REMEMBER...............................Maria Schmidt ..105
    Looking Back

19. S = Seeing...Judy Deppman ..112
    Seeing With Unseeing Eyes

20. T = TRAVEL ....Cleona Ternes ..117
    Have Suitcase, Will Travel

21. U = USE YOUR TALENTS ....Burnett "Ben" Dirks ..123
    Releasing The Beauty Within

22. V = VOLUNTEER ....Gladys Barnes ..129
    Friendship Makes A Happy Heart

23. W = WRITE, WORK..............................Mark Johnson ..134
    Faithful Worker, Talented Writer

24. X = 'XPECT..Jack Williams ..140
    Keep Your Sense Of Humor

25. Y = YOU..Ellen Shay ..147
    You Are Your Own Best Friend

26. Z = ZEST...Wilma York ..155
    Living Life To The Fullest

Lessons I Have Learned From My A To Z Friends........161

I dedicate Positive Aging *to you, my readers; I have written every word with you in mind. It is my sincere wish that your older years will be enriched by the lessons we have learned from my wise friends.*

Acknowledgments

My first acknowledgment is to my Maker who blessed me with a desire to learn and a curiosity about what makes me who I am. I acknowledge my Maker for giving me the audacity to ask people to share their life stories, knowing I would tell the whole world.

I acknowledge myself for having the persistence to stick with it even when I asked, "Why?"

My heart-felt thanks to my friends and their loved ones for allowing me to tell their inspiring stories. There would be no book without those twenty-six positive agers.

Thanks to my professors at Sonoma State University for teaching me about aging and other things. An extra-special thanks to Susan Hillier, Ph.D., my professor, friend and mentor.

Thank you to my family, my good friends and acquaintances who have been most supportive. They saw in me an example of aging positively and believed I could write a book.

Preface

The invitation I held in my hand clearly said, "You are invited to attend the 50th anniversary reunion of the class of 1936." Could it be possible that it had been fifty years since I graduated from high school? How had those fifty years slipped by so quickly? How had that pretty, young girl-graduate become the mature woman I see in my mirror today?

Fifty years ago I could not imagine myself being old—I believed I would always be young. My grandparents were old, but they must always have been old; surely they were never young like me. I had to think about this—How had I become my grandparents' age?

Since that invitation arrived, I have looked back over those fifty years and have become aware that my aging has been a process of living one day at a time—I did not grow old overnight or in one quantum leap. I have learned, also, that I will probably live longer than my grandparents lived. Because of medical discoveries and advances in health care, I can expect to live longer and better. Since their time, much has been learned about the process of aging and insights gained as to how our attitudes and perspectives affect our physical, mental, and emotional health. Professionals in the health and social fields now know that we, as individuals, can do much to increase the number of our years and, more importantly, that we can add quality to those extra years.

Each year brings opportunities and benefits inherent with growing older. Those opportunities and benefits must be recognized and worked at just as does any successful enterprise. We cannot sit in our rocking chairs, twiddling our thumbs, waiting for good things to happen; we must take responsibility for making them happen. As infants we did not sit on our bottoms and learn to walk—we got up, fell down, and got up again until we had mastered the art of walking. We did not learn to read by wishing we could—we learned to read one word at a time. In much the same way we can assure the success of our older years through our own determination, energy, and persistence.

With each added year comes wisdom and maturity gained through experience. Aging is inevitable, a natural consequence of living; we can accept it as a friend or we can fear it as an enemy. Old age does not have to be a dreaded never-never land; it can be a time to let go of responsibilities, a time to remember, and a time to enjoy life. It is up to each of us to decide to accept old age as reward or as punishment. We can regret the passing years or we can expand our horizons and look forward to new experiences.

Positive Aging was born out of classes I took when I returned to college at the age of sixty-eight. My children were grown; I had retired from the business world, and I was determined not to spend my days rocking, reading, and watching television; I believed there was still much for me to learn and to experience. As I studied about the aging process, I realized that I was enjoying the richness of my older years and that I might be able to help others know that their later years can be some of their best.

To obtain material beyond my own experiences, I interviewed twenty-six people (A to Z) and wrote brief stories of their lives, emphasizing the qualities which made each one a role model for aging positively. I had the privilege of face-to-face conversations with most of them; some I have known for many years; others I have met in various ways. The stories of those no longer living were told to me by family members who are proud of their loved ones and happy to share their stories.

As I have looked back over those fifty years the invitation asked me to celebrate, I have found some answers for how that young girl became the woman I am today. I realize that my aging has been a day-to-day process in which I have had many rich experiences—some I labeled "good" and some I labeled "bad"—all contributing to my growing older. It is those experiences which have changed that young graduate into the woman I am today. It is indeed a time to celebrate.

The Aging Party

My friend asked me, "What will you wear to the party?"
    The Aging Party.
I love parties and I wanted to be well-dressed.
I looked in my closet.
What would be appropriate to wear to an Aging Party?
I could wear this grey dress of Conformity.
    But I've worn it to so many parties.
I could wear these sensible shoes of Thriftiness.
    But they are too tight; they hurt my feet.
    I need dancing shoes for this party.
This cloth coat of Stability will be warm for the
evening air.
    No, it is time I bought a new coat for the occasion.
What shall I wear to the Party?
I've worn these old clothes far too long.
    I need a new wardrobe.

I thought and I planned.
This was a special party; it called for special clothes.
    My old ones just would not do.

I shopped today.
I bought a bright red dress of Adventure.
    It is really very Daring.
The hat I bought!
I threw away my modest little pillbox.
My new hat has a broad brim of Self-Confidence
    Trimmed with a scarlet flower of Assurance
    And a checkered band of Optimism.
My new shoes are perfect for dancing.

They are made of sunshine with a rainbow for
   trimming.
I have replaced my coat of Stability.
My new one has threads of exquisite Extravagance
   Buttoned with buttons of Beauty.

My new clothes are ready.
But what shall I do with my hair?
I've worn this neat, perfectly coiffed style for many
years.
   Nothing else would be "me."
I'll be reckless! I'll release my hair to Freedom.
   I'll wear a fringe of Friendship curls.
   And color it with moonbeams.

   My new makeup will be a smile
   With a sparkle in my eyes.

I'm ready for the party.
I'm filled with Confidence.
   I know I look Beautiful.

Kay Drikey

*This piece of writing came to me on the wings of inspiration
at 3:00AM one April morning. I climbed out of bed, turned on
the light, located pen and paper, crawled back in bed, propped
myself on one elbow, and wrote it down before it could escape.*

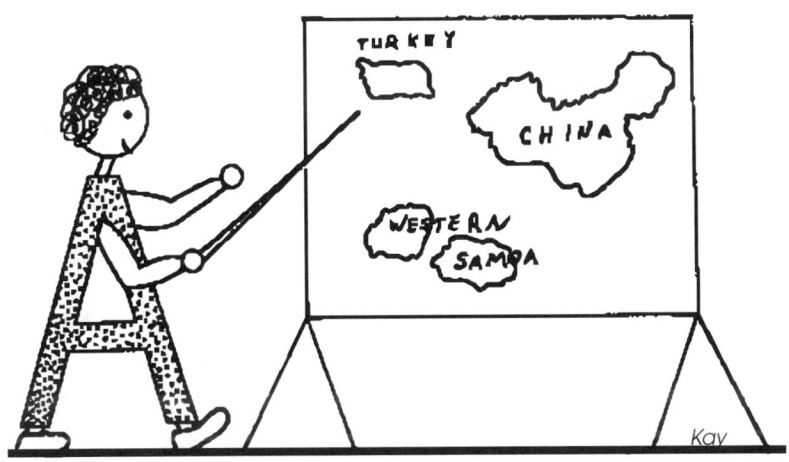

1. You Can't Give Love Away ...It Comes Back Tomorrow

Interesting conversation, enthusiasm and caring, as well as delicious food, are enjoyed every meal at Pilgrim Place, a retirement residence in Southern California. Doris Hauser is one of the enthusiastic, caring people who shares stories of her interesting life with the other residents, all of whom have been involved in some way with the Congregational Church. Doris' husband was a Congregational minister for many years and Doris, as the minister's wife, worked in various and sundry capacities in every parish where he served. Her husband died in 1982, ending their marriage of 44 years.

After her husband's death, Doris sold their large

home and bought her own small house with a tiny backyard and patio where she enjoys sharing her morning coffee with her friends or just basking in the sunshine as she reads the morning paper—if she has time for such a leisurely activity. Inside Doris' home are souvenirs collected on her travels. On one wall hangs a hand-woven mat from Western Samoa; tables and shelves hold art objects from China and Turkey, as well as a tiny replica of a Samoan "fale" (house).

When she had been widowed for a year, Doris joined the Peace Corps. She was 66. Her Peace Corps assignment sent her to Apia, Western Samoa, where she taught English at the Congregational High School. Those two years were packed with adventure. She loved the Samoan people, developed many friendships, and goes back every few years to visit those friends and experience again the beauty of the islands.

Doris believes that "older persons have skills badly needed in under-developed countries and they should know that the Peace Corps takes good care of its volunteers—of any age." Her two years in Western Samoa convinced her of the value of the Peace Corps goal of helping people help themselves.

Doris put on her traveling shoes again when she went with friends on a "People to People Tour" of China. "When I returned from that trip," Doris says, "I needed structure in my living." To meet this need, she taught English as a Second Language at a high school in a nearby city.

Tarsus, Turkey, was the site of Doris' next adventure; she went to Turkey as an English teacher when she made the decision "to collect adventures instead of salary checks."

When the Peace Corps came knocking on Doris' door again, she was tempted to answer the call; however, her family and friends convinced her that she could still serve, "collect adventures," and stay at home. They were particularly concerned for Doris' health because she had fractured her back in Samoa when she slipped on lava, and she had been "knocked down by a big, big dog in Germany en route home from Turkey." As a result of those "misadventures," she wears a body brace which she calls her "Space Suit."

When she was finally convinced that she could serve at home as well as abroad, Doris became a teacher with Volunteer Vital English (VVE). Her first students were two mothers from Mexico, their five children, and "an assortment of brothers who spoke limited English." She not only taught them English, she took one of their babies, who cried constantly, to her own doctor for treatment since the family had no way to get help.

Doris' small home is a home-away-from-home and classroom for people from many countries. She counts her many blessings and declares, "There's all that plus a chance to volunteer full time and receive copious love from Indonesians, Sudanese, Jordanians, Japanese, Koreans, and Brazilians; but the students from the People's Republic of China are most visible. So I provide the food—they cook. English-Spoken-Here is the rule! I listen, I care, I give love. . . . I've found out that you can't give love away. It comes back tomorrow."

Doris sums up her adventures with these words: "I don't see how we can have wars if you like people . . . if you like them enough, you learn to love them."

A = Adventure

Adventure! It makes life worth living! Some in our youth-oriented society believe there is an unwritten law which legislates that adventure belongs only to the young. Don't you believe it! Adventure can be the "stuff" of old age; it can give the later years a sparkle, an aliveness.

The dictionary defines "adventure" as "a bold undertaking, in which hazards are to be met; a daring feat." That is what living and aging are—bold undertakings and daring feats. It is impossible to travel the road from infancy to old age without meeting hazards on the way. Daring to meet those obstacles head-on and overcoming them add to the adventure of aging.

One of the myths of aging is that older people lose the courage to take risks, that they are set in their ways and are no longer interested in anything new and different. The lives of numerous seniors prove this is only a myth. Some of my favorite stories are those of pioneers crossing the plains in covered wagons. Not all of the early settlers were young; many were older people with a sense of adventure and a burning desire for a new life; that desire gave them the courage to risk leaving their familiar lives in search of new experiences.

When we were children, our lives were one big happening; we built sand castles, tried to dig a hole deep enough to reach China, tried to fly like a bird, and we were sure we could jump over tall buildings like Superman. We may not find digging a hole to China or jumping over buildings something we would like to try today, but we can find adventure by leaving well-beaten paths to explore the less-traveled byways. Wonderful books have been written by and about older people who have had the courage to explore.

I keep a scrapbook in which I collect stories about seniors who refuse to think themselves into old age. Among the stories is one of a 74-year-old woman who climbed to the top of Mt. Kilimanjaro. Another is that of a husband and wife team, both past 70 and described as two vibrant, energetic people, who win swimming championships.

Living adventurously does not have to be a physical experience and it does not require a large travel budget. Luxurious cruise ships and hi-tech airliners are not needed to enjoy new experiences. An armchair, a wheelchair, or even a hospital bed, can serve as a launching pad. The vehicle can be a book, a television set, or a radio. We can see foreign countries and meet people of many races through words and pictures; we can even travel through space via pictures sent back to earth by satellite.

A friend sent me the following article which is signed "Rosalie." I don't know Rosalie, but I like her philosophy:

If I Had My Life to Live Over

I would climb more mountains, swim more rivers, and watch more sunsets. I would eat more ice cream and less spinach. I would have more troubles and fewer imaginary ones.

You see, I am one of those people who lives sensibly and sanely, hour after hour, day by day. Oh, I've had my moments . . . and, if I had it to do over again, I'd have lots more of them. In fact, I'd have nothing else. Just moments, one after another, instead of living so many years ahead each day. I have been one of those people who was afraid to take a chance, afraid to make a mistake, afraid of being hurt, afraid to make my dreams too big.

If I had it to do over again, I would go places, and do things and travel lighter than I have. If I had my life to live over, I would start barefooted earlier in the spring and stay that way longer in the fall. I would work harder and play harder and cram my life full of beautiful memories.

I would ride on more merry-go-rounds.

I'd pick more daisies.

Rosalie

If we, like Rosalie, are "one of those people who lives sensibly and sanely, hour after hour, day by day," maybe it is time to be flexible, to take risks. We can begin by seeking new experiences, even if we cannot climb a mountain or be a champion swimmer. We can be interested in other people's adventures; we can read, watch, and use our imaginations. We can *make* our lives an adventure.

B = Bloom

Kay

2. Small In Stature Large In Courage

Luella Wood was almost 87 when she moved from Lincoln, Nebraska to Southern California. That may not sound like a great accomplishment until you learn that she made all of the arrangements, did all of the packing, sold the things she could not move–all by herself. Luella was small in stature but large in courage. Whatever Life handed her, she handled. She found a way to bloom where she was planted.

Luella was born in a sod house on a farm in Nebraska, the second child in a family of five girls and two boys. She married a young farmer when she was

7

twenty; when they had been married twelve years (she was thirty-two and he was thirty-four) he died suddenly of a heart attack, leaving her with five daughters, the youngest only three years old. Luella's parents opened their hearts and their farm home to the fatherless family. It was difficult for Luella to be the only parent, and that difficulty was compounded by the Depression and by living in the Dust Bowl of Nebraska. She wrote in her memoirs, "The worst time was during the drought in the 1930s. I don't like to think of those summers. It was so dry and hot and windy and dust everywhere."

Sometimes Luella found it almost impossible to see any future hope for her girls. It seemed almost a miracle when a generous cousin in California offered to help each daughter get a higher education after she graduated from high school. One by one, they moved to California. Luella described her feelings: "It is hard to give up your girls at that age and not see them for a year or longer. But I always said to myself, 'All things work together for good to those who love the Lord.'" Luella's faith was the secret that enabled her to continue to make a home for herself and her girls in spite of overwhelming odds.

At fifty-three, Luella passed a Civil Service examination and began working for the State of Nebraska as a clerk-typist. She had learned to type by taking classes at night school just in time to pass the test. She worked in the State Capitol in Lincoln, Nebraska, for sixteen years; she liked being part of the business world.

Luella retired at sixty-nine, then she went back for three years on a temporary basis. When she retired permanently, she worked as a baby-sitter to eke out a living on her small pension and Social Security.

The cold, ice, and snow of Nebraska's winters finally convinced Luella that she should move to the warmer climate of Southern California. There she and her oldest daughter shared an apartment in a Retirement Center. Although she was glad to be near her daughters, sons-in-law, and grandchildren, she was homesick for the sight of the Nebraska State Capitol where she had spent so many years. She missed the good friends she had left behind in Nebraska. In her special way, however, Luella adjusted and summed up her experience: "When I look back, I know God led me here in all of this move. It is so wonderful to be near my family. I miss Nebraska but it is good to miss the cold and ice and to be able to see flowers blooming in the yards all year around."

Luella died suddenly on March 2, 1989; she would have been 93 in May. She had enjoyed that day—she walked to the dining room for all three meals, talked with friends, and was enjoying a visit with a granddaughter when death suddenly claimed her.

Luella's friends and family gathered to honor her at a memorial service in her California home; even more friends and family attended a service for her in the Nebraska town where she was born, where her children were born, where she spent most of her life, and where she is buried. Her pleasant personality and caring attitude are remembered by everyone her life touched. She left a loving legacy for those five daughters, her eight grandchildren and five great-grandchildren.

These words were not written by a stranger; I am one of the five daughters to whom Mother left a rich legacy— she didn't leave us antiques and fine china; she left us more —she left us the challenge to make the most of life in spite of the obstacles and to believe that, "All things work together for good to those who love the Lord." She left us the challenge to bloom where we are planted.

B = Bloom

To bloom in nature is to produce or yield a blossom. Blooming is bursting free and becoming more. We are free to choose to bloom—burst free of our circumstances and grow—or to refuse to bloom and let circumstances dictate the course of our lives.

Absolutely everyone—no exceptions—meets challenges on life's journey. Some accept those challenges as opportunities to become wiser and stronger, while others declare, "It wasn't my fault," and do nothing to help themselves.

Blooming is not always easy; sometimes life deals us heavy blows, but we can handle those blows if we maintain our courage and meet our challenges head-on. If we decide to make the best of circumstances, we win; if we let circumstances dictate how we live, we lose. Those who choose to bloom are happy people; their company is sought by others; they feel good about themselves; and they look forward to each new day with eager anticipation.

Several years ago, I met Mildred Vandenburgh, author of *Fill Your Days With Life*.[1] Mildred wrote her story to tell others how she learned to fill her days with life in spite of challenges and disappointments—how she bloomed where she was planted. Singing had

---

1 Vandenburgh, Mildred. *Fill your Days With Life*. Regal Books Division, G. L. Publications, Glendale, CA, 1975.

been a vital part of Mildred's younger years; she had been a lyric soprano and had sung as soloist; she had directed choirs and glee clubs. When her family was grown and she had retired, Mildred could hardly wait to begin singing again. She finally had the time. Even the rainy evening couldn't stop her from going to choir practice for the first time.

"I didn't expect solo parts at first," Mildred confesses, "I was willing to volunteer my expertise to choral work until I got back 'in voice'." Her hopes were shattered, however, at the end of the practice session when the choir director announced, "Voices change when you don't use them. Trying to join a choir after forty doesn't work out." Mildred was sixty-five.

Mildred was shocked and angry and sure the choir director was mistaken; she would prove it. Day after day, she practiced by recording her voice and playing it back. The choir director was right; her voice was not the voice she remembered. Mildred's ego was bruised. She was hurt and angry and defeated for several days until her neighbor called to invite her to participate in other activities at the church. She reluctantly accepted her neighbor's invitation and before long Mildred was blooming again. She organized and directed a harmonica choir and played the piano for Sunday School classes. When she chose to bloom where she was planted, her life took on new meaning and she felt she had a new reason to live.

Luella and Mildred did nothing the rest of us cannot do. We, too, can bloom when we have the courage and determination to meet every challenge. We can expect to make new friends and have interesting experiences in whatever circumstances we find ourselves.

C = Communicate

Kay

3. Turning Retire-ment Into Living-ment

"I've been a writer much of my adult life—I have had six books published; I am working on my seventh, and there are still more I want to write." At an age when most people are enjoying retire-ment, Dorothy Loa Bruegger is enjoying living-ment.

Dorothy wrote her first six books on a typewriter; now, however, being the up-to-date author that she is, she uses a Macintosh computer which she bought and learned to use when she was eighty-four. "I adopted the computer," Dorothy says, "because my eyesight was deteriorating; I couldn't see what I had written on the typewriter, the type was so small. On the computer I could use larger type." Learning to use her computer was a challenge, but Dorothy thrives on challenges. She mastered her computer and today she uses the jargon as well as any young computer whiz, and she encourages other older people to buy one and learn to use it.

Dorothy lives in a retirement home where she produces a 14-page, in-house bi-monthly newsletter on her trusty Mac. She uses it to write a personal letter, around Thanksgiving each year, to two hundred relatives and friends.

Dorothy and her husband Jim were amateur photographers who traveled extensively. As they traveled, they specialized in photographing gardens and used their pictures to illustrate three books they wrote— *Touring the Gardens of Europe*; *Gardens of Europe, a Pictorial Tour*; and *Oriental Gardens in America, A Visitor's Guide*. They also gave slide lectures.

Dorothy and Jim were married fifty-three years when he died. Dorothy then married Fred, another photographer, who lived only four more years. Dorothy remembers, "We had four very happy years photographing together—and laughing a lot."

In addition to her six books, more than one hundred of Dorothy's articles have been published in such magazines as *Bon Appetit*, *The Garden*, *House Beautiful*, *Travel*, and *Westways*. She also edited and conducted a series of children's television programs on CBS. She founded a touring theater for child audiences which took plays, operas, and spoken ballets, done by adult professionals, to four million children in forty states.

Dorothy's name appears in a number of WHO'S

WHO listings; she was past eighty when she was elected Woman of Achievement by her chapter of the National League of American Pen Women.

It is astonishing to learn, considering the extent of Dorothy's accomplishments, that she does not have a college degree. She recalls that she passed her entrance exams for Vassar but chose marriage instead.

Although she is "pushing ninety" (her words), Dorothy continues to write. A literary agent is standing by, ready to sell her next book as soon as she finishes writing it. Her new book "is a new kind of garden book featuring the creative people who produced twelve fine gardens in Europe." As with her other books, Dorothy will illustrate this one with pictures she has taken.

Dorothy doesn't sit and worry about growing old. She is busy writing, attending Elderhostels, and enjoying "fine evening programs I can see on television— especially the MacNeil-Lehrer News Hour, Bill Moyer's fabulous challenging interviews, the delightful Nova nature programs, National Geographic specials, Smithsonian Institute travelogs—what a wealth of stimulating, sometimes agonizing, news and information, and happy recognition of scenes I knew on our travels!" She is grateful "to be able to bring so much from the outer world into my little cottage!"

Dorothy has learned valuable lessons in the years she has lived and has sage advice for the rest of us; she suggests that we can make our lives more meaningful if we "find some way to focus on others, to help others." Following her advice will assure that we, like Dorothy, are too busy to worry about the passing years.

C = Communicate

Communication is:
    Exchanging information
      Conveying meaning
        Breaking barriers
          Sharing with others
            Opening doors.
Communication is:
    Talking
      Writing
        Touching
          Listening
            Smiling, frowning
              Accepting, rejecting.

Good communication is important to starting and keeping healthy and rewarding relationships; it is a skill that takes practice, sensitivity, and thought. There is always a need to communicate, for no person lives completely alone. Our ability to communicate enables us to live harmoniously with others; we can work effectively together when we exchange ideas and feelings. In honest communication we let the other into the inner recesses of our being by sharing our feelings, our needs, and our desires.

Communication is a vital part of life from birth to death. As a tiny baby we do not understand words and cannot speak them; however, we can communicate in other ways. We come into this world with an innate understanding of touch. No one has to teach us that a gentle touch communicates approval and acceptance, while a blow or slap communicates disapproval and rejection. Even in the first months of life we recognize the difference between a smile and a frown. As infants, we can express ourselves in still another way without the use of words. Our first lusty yell at birth is our way of telling those around us how we feel and what we need. It works every time.

As we grow older, we learn to use words and a new world is opened to us. We soon become experts at selecting the right word to fit each occasion. We learn to ask questions, to give answers, to thank, to blame, and to express love or hate. We also communicate through actions, gestures, tone of voice, a twinkle in the eye, a smile or a frown. According to an old adage, "Our actions speak louder than our words."

Although most communication is accomplished through words and actions, communication is even more—it is listening. There is no communication unless someone is listening.

Other communication tools are books, magazines, newspapers, radio, and television—all links to the outside world for people who are not able to leave their homes.

Talking, listening, writing—all these are only tools of communication. True communication results from sharing feelings. No matter how many intellectual and descriptive words we use, they mean nothing unless they sincerely express our feelings; people respond more to feelings than to words.

Regardless of what communication avenue we choose to use, most of us who are past sixty would tell others that we are not unhappy. We have lived full lives, have had exciting experiences, and have met interesting people. We have climbed mountains and walked through valleys; we have met challenges and accepted responsibilities. Now we are ready to enjoy our rich harvest of memories. We know and choose to communicate that aging can be an interesting experience, and it is up to us to make it so.

D = Dare

Kay

4. Still Cruising At 109

"I'll see you here next year for another ride."
"I'll plan on it."

The man in charge of the rides at the Wildlife Safari had just helped Nina Rust dismount and he invited her to come back for another ride one year later. Nina accepted the invitation.

Nina is no ordinary woman and that was no ordinary ride. Nina was celebrating her 99th birthday by riding on the back of a gigantic African elephant.

True to her word, Nina was back one year later to celebrate her 100th birthday with another elephant ride. But she didn't stop there—riding an elephant became a habit; she rode again, accompanied by her 81-year-old daughter, when she was 103 and 104.

Let's go back to the beginning of Nina's long life. She was born in 1881 in a sod house on a homestead in Nebraska, one of nine children. She married Sam Rust when she was twenty-one and gave birth to twelve children.

Sam was never robust, which meant that Nina had to help earn the money to raise their large family. Because she needed to work at home while watching her children, she took in washing and sewed for other people as well as for her own family. She also sewed as part of a WPA (Works Progress Administration) project. When there was no money to buy material, she made her children's clothes out of flour sacks.

As she contended with her own twelve pregnancies and bouts of morning sickness, Nina showed almost Herculean strength in helping her husband and children recover from rattlesnake bites, influenza and pneumonia. It is hard to imagine how she found the time and energy to plant a large garden each year and to can hundreds of quarts of fruits and vegetables, but she did.

When Nina and Sam had been married 41 years, Sam died. Nina's official home, after Sam's death, was with a daughter; nevertheless, she was always ready to go wherever she was needed. Even the distance she had to travel, mostly by bus, didn't stop her from being there when her grandchildren, her great-grandchildren, and even her great-great-grandchildren were born.

Riding an elephant on her 99th birthday was only

one of the ways Nina Rust proved that she was never too old to do anything she made up her mind to do; she didn't wait until she was 99 or 100 to defy the laws of aging. According to her daughter, when Nina was a youngster of 63 she "decided to lay the new linoleum rug on the kitchen floor. Somehow she managed to raise the stove and put the linoleum under it all by herself, afterwards wondering how she had done it."[1]

The year Nina turned 82, she "went fishing a lot that summer." On her 84th birthday, an 11-year-old neighbor boy came to play croquet with Nina. She was still a kid at heart.

When Nina was 94 she took over the cooking and housework when her daughter was sick for several months. About that time, Nina learned that she was a borderline diabetic. When the doctor asked her if she ever got short of breath, she answered, "Well, if I'd run uphill I would." She has never lost her sense of humor and her love for games, puzzles, and playing cards.

At 96, Nina was still hooking rugs; that year she finished her masterpiece—a map of the United States about 30 inches by 50 inches, which she designed herself from a road map.

Along with all the publicity that accompanied Nina's 100th birthday, she received a gift of her first airplane ride. In true Nina-fashion, she enjoyed the ride from take-off to landing.

Just a few days before her 101st birthday, Nina took her first jet plane ride. Whenever she had to change

---

1 McMeekin, Phyllis. *Dear Reader, 100 Years with Nina Rust.* Graphic Dimensions, Roseburg, OR, 1984.

planes, the stewardess wanted to get a wheelchair for her, but the plucky Nina refused, explaining that she would ride in a wheelchair when she was old, and not before.

In June 1990, Nina celebrated her 109th birthday with a picnic at the scene of her elephant ride ten years before. She declined to ride an elephant on this occasions because "it was too bumpy."

There is no stopping Nina! Three months after her 109th birthday, Nina rode proudly in the lead car in a classic car parade in Roseburg, Oregon. As reported in the Roseburg News Review, "Nina was dressed in a hot pink T-shirt. She and her date (her grandson) rolled down Roseburg's main drag in a cool, white 1957 Chevy Bel Air two-door hardtop." Her grandson had made a sign for the side of the car; it read "109 and still cruising." The picture accompanying the story shows Nina waving at the crowd.

Nina's life story is positive proof that life can be full and happy if we make it that way. She has not let growing old dictate how she will live; she just keeps busy doing for others and finding new ways to enjoy life.

D = Dare

"Aging" and "daring" are two words not often found in the same sentence; in my opinion, however, they belong together—aging successfully requires daring.

Most of us—young and old alike—believe we would choose to live challenge-free lives. In reality, there is no such thing as a challenge-free life, and if there were, it would not be a life worth living. Challenges add spice to life.

One of the myths of aging is that older people lose

their willingness to dare, that they are set in their ways and are no longer interested in anything new and different. The lives of many seniors prove that this is only myth. Nina Rust would not have ridden an elephant at ages 99, 100, 103 and 104, or taken her first airplane ride at 100 and first jet ride at 101 if she had not been a darer.

In my scrapbook on *Positive Aging* are many examples of daring. One is the story of a man who took up hang gliding when he was 72 and has ridden currents as high as 2,500 feet and as long as an hour. Another is the story of the Polar Bear Club whose senior members dare to swim in the frigid ocean near San Francisco every New Year's Day. Older people living in Germany in World War II risked their lives by giving refuge to Jews; few of us are challenged to have that much courage.

Just as no one can live our lives for us, no one can dare for us. No one can experience the power and satisfaction we feel when we dare to ignore the myth that old people are afraid to seek new adventures and experiences. We know what gives meaning to life and we are willing to take risks to make our lives richer.

Some wise person said it best in these words: "A Butterfly Is Just A Caterpillar That Took A Chance." Maybe we who are no longer young should call ourselves the Butterfly Generation. We were caterpillars who dared to take a chance.

E = Enjoy

Kay

5. Dancing Through Life

Her name should have been "Joy," but how were her parents to know what a laughing, dancing, loving person she would be when they named her "Edith"?

Edith "Edie" Morrison, a native Californian, was born with her dancing shoes on. She had no formal dancing lessons, but she danced!—from early childhood until six months before she died at the age of ninety.

Edie lived through the rigors of the Depression; she dropped out of school before she finished high school, and raised her daughter, Betty, by herself, supporting her by working as a waitress. Her love of dancing helped her through the rough times as she glided

23

gracefully to the music of the Big Bands whenever they played in San Francisco.

When Edie was very young she worked in a candy store, and, according to Betty, "she thought that was the sweetest place to work." When she was past fifty she still had the sweetness of the candy store in her mind and decided to realize her life-long dream by opening her own candy store, Kandy Kottage. Betty and her two young daughters worked with her to create a unique store; they wore ruffles, bonnets and pantaloons and presented puppet shows; a gingerbread fence was part of the decor. They concocted fancy ice cream dishes and called them Peter Pan Sundaes and Cinderella Banana Splits. Even when they worked hard, they had fun. They made a profit in their small resort town during the tourist season; however, that season was too short and the rent was too high. After three years, Edie had to admit that fun wasn't paying the bills and she reluctantly closed her Kandy Kottage.

Soon after giving up her dream, Edie suffered a stroke, but she was not defeated. She went to live with Betty while she recovered, and she was soon dancing again. Edie was a student of Religious Science which taught her that she was responsible for her own life, and she was determined to live a life of fun and dancing, not one of sickness and inactivity.

It is beautiful to hear the kind and loving words Betty has to say about her mother. "Edie got along with everyone. All who ever knew her were inspired by her congeniality and lovingness; she was generous with her hugs and kisses. She never knew anyone's age because age wasn't important to her; she was ageless and she saw everyone else as ageless."

Edie was style conscious. Because she was tiny, vivacious and cute, any style was right for her and she was able to dress tastefully like a 20-year-old when she was eighty. Her 102 pounds and 4' 11" figure allowed her to wear whatever was the fashion at the moment—pants, shorts, skirts—long, short, or in-between.

Square dancing and waltzing were Edie's first loves; she and her husband Joe were experts in both. When they waltzed, the other dancers stood back to watch and admire. She and Joe traveled many miles to attend square dance gatherings where Edie enjoyed showing off her wardrobe of square-dance dresses, full petticoats and dancing shoes.

A new and exciting phase of Edie's life began when she became an important member of a Fun-After-50 senior group organized by Betty. From that group was born the Kitchen Kut-Ups which started as a kazoo band and grew to be a dance review troupe presenting elaborate routines complete with costumes and special lighting. Although Edie was seventy when the Kitchen Kut-Ups were organized, she was the star from that day on.

For fifteen years Edie performed with the Kitchen Kut-Ups in their annual, highly professional, Razzle Dazzle show. In her final appearance, when she was eighty-nine, Edie was featured in nine different numbers with nine complicated costume changes, all packed into a three-hour show. Betty says proudly, "She danced and she did comedy. She could remember every routine. Her memory was excellent right up to the end."

According to Betty, "Mother would try anything—absolutely anything. She and Joe went to Hawaii twelve times after she was seventy, usually to dance with a square dance group. She loved Hawaii and she loved square dancing."

Although Betty makes most of the costumes for the dance reviews, Edie sewed her own. She dressed as a chicken, a clown, a Can-Can dancer, a princess, and other characters. "Her sense of style was most helpful; she just knew what would be attractive for different people."

Edie loved fun. Everything was fun. She taught Betty, "As long as it was fun, it was probably O.K. Music was fun and dancing was fun. She was a happy-go-lucky person."

Just three days after her last performance, Edie had a stroke. She had been sick with cancer, but no one knew how sick she was. It didn't stop her—the show must go on!

Her family and friends paid a special tribute to Edie after her death. Because they knew she would not like a sad and gloomy funeral, they planned a celebration at a local recreation center; pictures of Edie in her beautiful ruffled, ribboned, feathered, and sequined costumes were everywhere. They played a video of Edie in all of her dances for the last five years. The man who has played the piano for their group for seventeen years played a medley of many of the songs to which Edie had danced. They ate and drank at Edie's party and kept the celebration in a light vein just as they knew she would want it.

Edie's love of fun and dancing lives on in her daughter, her son-in-law, her two granddaughters, and her two great-grandsons. When one great-grandson was about four he saw Edie in her beautiful sequined costume; his wide eyes opened even wider as he exclaimed, "Oh, you are my fairy grandmother!" She was indeed a "fairy grandmother"—a glamorous grandmother who dressed in bright and sparkling clothes.

Betty's admiration for her mother comes through loud and clear in her tribute—"She was quite a lady!"

E = Enjoy

To enjoy means "to have satisfaction in experiencing." The very word "joy" fairly sparkles; it denotes happiness, the expectation of good, gladness, delight. No life can have too much joy.

In the past, many in our youth-oriented society believed that joy belonged exclusively to those under thirty; that the younger years were joy-filled and the older years were joy-empty. We now know that our older years can be some of our most enjoyable because joy is not measured by years. We can decide how we want to experience our older years; joy or no joy depend on our attitudes, our beliefs, and our expectations.

How can we ensure that our mature years will be joy-filled? One way is by learning all we can about aging while we are young. We can know older people and learn what makes them happy. If we make the most of life when we are young, we will continue to make the most of life when we are old. Look for the beauty in people; look beyond their appearance, both in youth and in old age.

If we have already reached the years which society has labeled "joy-empty", we can still learn to fill the "joy-tank." We can spend our time with people who see the bright side of life and spend little or no time with those whose main topics of conversation are their ailments and what they are no longer able to do. By spending time with folks who love and accept themselves, we will learn to love and accept ourselves, and others will want to be around us. We need to remember, however, that we can learn from others, but ultimately we have to find the joy within ourselves.

Although young people may not believe it, there are advantages to being old—we are free from many former responsibilities and we have more hours to spend on projects and programs of our choice. We no longer need to worry about reaching the top of the corporate ladder. We don't need to be concerned about status or the opinion of others. We can finally be ourselves.

A sense of humor is as good as any anti-aging cream on the market. My Aunt Orene is ninety and moves a bit slower than she did fifty years ago, but her sense of humor and her love of laughter still delight her family, friends, nieces, and nephews. She always has a joke, a cartoon, or an amusing anecdote to share. She keeps her sense of humor watered daily so that it doesn't have a chance to dry up.

A small paperback entitled 14,000 *Things To Be Happy About*,[1] lists pages and pages of everyday, simple experiences which we may not have thought of as sources of joy. We can make our own lists of "things to be happy about"—things we can relish and feast on; things we can take pleasure in, delight in, and love.

We may not be able to dance when we are ninety, as Edie did, but we can find our own ways to experience joy. We only need to remind ourselves that joy doesn't know the difference between nine and ninety.

---

1 Kipfer, Barbara Ann. 14,000 *Things To Be Happy About.* Workman Publishing, New York, NY, 1990.

F = Friendship

Kay

6. Accentuate The Positive

When Sumner "Pax" Paxson says, "You can turn an experience from negative to positive if you work at it," you had better listen because Pax knows what he is talking about.

Pax lives in a convalescent hospital where he has been a resident for eight years. He shares a small room with another man; every earthly possession Pax owns is crowded into his half of the room. In spite of his limited space, Pax says he is a happy man and he is glad to call the half-room "home."

Pax has known many negatives in his 73 years, some of which have been devastating; however, through hard work and determination, he has turned those negatives into positives.

The Depression was at its height when it was time for Pax to go to college, and there was no money for college; he went instead into the Civilian Conservation Corps (CCC). He says of his CCC experience, "I had a ball!" In addition to performing his assigned duties, Pax wrote letters for some of his fellow CCCers and taught English to others.

After he finished his stint in the CCC, Pax worked at various jobs: he worked in a sign shop, he was assistant manager of a theater, and he worked in a camera store.

Pax was happily married for twenty years. He and his wife devoted their lives to their two children until both teenagers were killed in a tragic car accident. His wife died two years later "of a broken heart."

Pax turned to drinking to drown his sorrows, often drinking himself into oblivion to relieve the pain. Several times he passed out on city streets and regained consciousness in an alley where he had been beaten and robbed of his money, his watch, and everything he owned. At one of his court appearances, a judge warned Pax that he would be sent to a prison farm if he came before that judge again, and that is just what happened.

While he was in prison, Pax learned that he could get out early if he donated blood; he did that and gained his freedom in twenty-five days. Those days in prison made Pax realize he had better do something to turn his life around; he was about as far down as he could go. He knew he had a serious drinking problem and needed to do something about it. Pax began attending Alcoholics Anonymous meetings which he credits with saving his life. But it wasn't easy;

it took several years of hard work and the help and encouragement of a good friend before Pax was able to stop drinking.

At last, life seemed to be going well for Pax; he was working regularly and he had made new friends. Unfortunately, that good life was not to last; Pax began having problems with his feet and was diagnosed as diabetic. Pax is grateful that he had a caring boss who fixed a place in the camera store for him to sit while he worked. His boss also paid for classes in accounting which allowed Pax to continue working at a job he could do while sitting.

In 1982, Pax's neighbors found him in his home in a diabetic coma; they called an ambulance to take him to an emergency hospital. When Pax regained consciousness, he found that doctors had amputated one leg and they recommended removal of the other. Pax refused to let them operate, and he will always be grateful that he regained consciousness in time to save his leg.

After Pax had endured five months of pain and skin grafts, hospital personnel decided to move him to the convalescent hospital which he calls "home" today.

Pax credits a "tough" physical therapist with freeing him from his prison of helplessness by insisting that he exercise and get out of bed. No matter how tough Pax tried to be, she was tougher. According to Pax, the most valuable lesson she taught him was how to get in and out of his wheelchair by himself. He also learned how to get in and out of a car, a skill which allows him to leave the hospital for shopping trips, speaking engagements, lunch or dinner "out." He appreciates the opportunity to get away at times, but insists, "It is always nice to get home."

A hospital staff member gets Pax's heartfelt thanks for suggesting that he take the CNA (Certified Nurse Assistant) course. He became the first hospital patient with one leg to earn that degree. Pax extended himself even further when he took the Hospital Chaplaincy course and became a Chaplain.

Pax has a pleasant and outgoing personality and is delighted when he is invited to speak before groups in the community. He has been honored for his accomplishments with Certificates of Recognition and a silver bowl which is proudly displayed at the hospital where he lives.

Pax is a special member of a group called LITA—Love Is The Answer. LITA is an organization for volunteers who establish a one-to-one friendship with hospital patients. According to LITA rules, each volunteer has only "one friend," but LITA has bent the rules for Pax who has twenty or more special friends. He is a true friend who feels it deeply when he loses one of his friends to death.

Pax has more than "people" friends—he also has "cat" friends. He feeds fifteen (or more) stray cats the leftover meat scraps and the extra milk which the kitchen workers save for him. The cats come regularly to the patio outside his room because they know there will always be a handout. He claims his cats are the fattest and healthiest cats around. Strangers who have heard about Pax and his cats call him the "cat man" and stop by to visit him and to see his cats. Several shelves in his limited space are filled with small ceramic cats and other knickknacks given to him by admiring friends.

On the walls of Pax's room are pictures of his friends, both human and feline. One is a picture of him playing Santa Claus at the hospital's Christmas party. He looks like the real thing in his red suit and cap, with a flowing white beard and white wig. Pax laughed when he said, "I didn't need anything in here, I have my own" as he patted his "bowl full of jelly."

Pax's story is an inspiration. He has worked through more tragedies than most people confront in a lifetime, and he has turned those negatives into positives. In Pax's words, "You can become an awful crank and a bore, or you can be a pleasant person to be around and I choose to be pleasant." He lives by those words as he extends his friendly hand.

F = Friendship

Our lives are enriched by our friendships. Friends are our alter egos, our other selves, our well-wishers and our sounding boards; friends care about us and we care about them; we grieve or rejoice with each other. The richest person is poor without friends; likewise, the poorest person is rich when he has friends. Friendship has no monetary value—it cannot be bought or sold; sincere friends love and respect each other for themselves alone.

True friendship is not a popularity contest; it is being honest with and feeling safe with another person. It is telling that person how much we value our relationship; it is being kind, spending time together, talking and listening. It is within the safe context of friendship that we can test new aspects of ourselves, that we can grow and develop.

Friends are a basic source of happiness. Preserving and nurturing our friendships should be at the top of our priority list. If we have lost track of a friend of former years, we should begin a search to find that person. We will find that doing the detective work can be exciting and when we find him, we have enriched both of our lives. Never let a good friend drift away.

Some believe it is more difficult to make new friends when we are older. I believe, however, if we are sincerely interested in others, we can make new friends at any age. It is our responsibility to make the first move; we cannot sit back and say, "People just aren't friendly anymore." Later life may, in fact, be the best time to establish new friendships—most of us have fewer responsibilities and more time to share, to talk, and to listen.

A natural part of aging is losing friends to death. Leo Buscaglia tells about losing an old friend: "To lose my dear friend after so many years of loving investment was terribly painful. It was difficult to part with such a positive force in my life. But nothing is forever. In reality we never lose the people we love. They become immortal through us. They continue to live in our hearts and minds. They participate in our every act, idea, and decision. No one will replace them and, in spite of the pain, we are richer for all the years invested in them. Because of them, we have so much more to bring to our relationships and those to come."[1]

Pax is a beautiful example of being a friend. He cares, he listens, and he is there when he is needed. We can follow Pax's example and have friends by being a friend.

---

1 Buscaglia, Leo. *Bus 9 to Paradise*. William Morrow and Co., Inc., New York, NY, 1986.

G = Give

Kay

7. Today's Elders Are Yesterday's Kids

On a beautiful sunny Northern California day, I interviewed Anna Stern in the home where she and her family have lived for thirty-five years. It didn't take long to observe that scholars live there—there are books everywhere! The library is lined with books from floor to ceiling; the shelves in Anna's office are full of books, and her son's room contains his library. Her husband is an opera buff who collects opera recordings to add to their library.

There are books on a wide variety of subjects.

Nursing has been Anna's career; not surprisingly, many of the books relate to nursing and medicine. She also has a special interest in the subject of aging; that interest accounts for another section of books. The whole family—mother, father, daughter, and son—have inquiring minds and an appreciation for music, art, and travel, all reflected on their book shelves.

Anna is of Slavic heritage and grew up in a Slavic community in Philadelphia. She learned to speak Ukrainian when she was seven and often helped her parents read and write letters for immigrant families. When she was still very young she was called upon to help women with medical problems by taking them to the dispensary and she helped immigrants to apply for their citizenship papers. This was her earliest volunteer work , about which she says, "I have been doing involuntary volunteer work for a long time, so when somebody asks me to do something, I do it." She has been a role model for her son and daughter who also work as volunteers.

Anna received her R.N. degree in 1935 in Hahnemann Medical College Hospital, School of Nursing, in Philadelphia. She had planned to be a doctor, but dropped the pre-med course and went into the Army Nurse Corps "because they were screaming for nurses." She spent much of her service time at sea on army transports. She met her husband when she was Chief Nurse and he, a Merchant Marine, was 2nd Officer on the same transport.

Anna retired from the service in 1950 with the rank of Captain. Her husband spent his career years in the Merchant Marines until he retired four years ago.

With her husband away much of the time, Anna

was busy making a home for their children. When the children were college age, she dropped much of the role of mother and assumed the role of classmate. She took history classes with her daughter and frequently ran into her son on campus. Anna was two years ahead of her daughter who was two ahead of her brother. Anna's nursing education came in handy; both children were taking anatomy and physics and the three of them were able to exchange ideas without being aware of their mother-child relationship or the difference in their ages.

Anna has always "operated under the premise that it is most important for me to keep mentally stimulated and to keep aware of new ideas." She acted on this premise by earning an A.A. when she was 57, a B.S. when she was 59, and her M.S. from University of California San Francisco when she was 63. Her Masters degree was Patho-Physiology with concentration in Gerontology. For four years following her graduation, she taught Gerontology and Continuing Education for Nurses at two of the colleges where she had been a student.

Anna has been active in civic affairs in her city and county. She has "always felt as a concerned adult I have an obligation to civic activities." She could paper her library with all of the certificates and honors she has received, most for her work in the field of aging. The California Nurses Association gave her an award which is especially meaningful to her; it is the "North Bay Coastal Region's Award for providing outstanding service to the community in general and the nursing community and elders in particular." She has a Certificate of Commendation for serving seven years on the County Commission on Aging. She is a guest speaker for the Area Agency on Aging (AAA) and she speaks at high schools and women's groups on positive aspects of aging. She belongs to the Women's Political Caucus and attended the President's White House Conference on Aging as a member of the County Committee. She served on the Steering Commission for the Buck Foundation, a new facility being built in Northern California for extensive research on aging.

The County Board of Supervisors presented Anna with a Certificate of Commendation for an Intergenerational Program which she developed and introduced in the school district. That program is designed to help young people better understand the elderly in order to build supportive relationships between the old and the young. Anna believes, "there should be an awareness that most older people are well and content and that for many, old age is a happy and productive time." The program also seeks "to prepare the young for their own aging so that they can recognize old age as a period of fulfillment toward which their entire life patterns are building. Through education about aging, thousands of youngsters are learning that all ages can benefit from one another. Most importantly, they are learning that today's elders are yesterday's kids and today's kids are tomorrow's elders."

After reading the list of Anna's achievements, you might think that she would have no time for her family, but that is not true; most family activities are planned around her two small grandchildren. The family home is still a gathering place for young people;

her son lives at home and his friends are always welcome. Anna say, "Having young people in the house guarantees that there will always be a great deal of stimulation and mental growth."

At the age of 74, when many older people are slowing down, Anna still sees much that needs to be done. She is especially anxious to get her Intergenerational Program integrated into all schools of the County. Maybe she will take some time for herself when that has been accomplished, but I wouldn't bet on it.

G = Give

A baby's wet kiss on a grandmother's soft cheek. A toddler's happy, "Do it again, Grandpa," as he bounces on grandfather's knee. Those are priceless gifts.

Ours is a gift-giving society. When we think of gifts, we too often think of material things; we forget that such simple things as a baby's kiss and a knee-bounce are also gifts. More important than the size or monetary value of the gift is the spirit in which it is given. "The gift without the giver is bare." Among my treasured gifts is a handprint picture my daughter made for me in her kindergarten class; the poems she wrote for me for Mother's Day are beyond price.

The greatest gift we can give is ourselves, our love, and our caring. When we give of ourselves without expecting anything in return we are truly blessed; we have given our very best gift.

There are many ways we can give: a smile doesn't cost a penny and very little effort—it is just a simple curving of the lips which can brighten someone's day. A smile conveys love, understanding, and acceptance.

Other gifts we can give are:
Sincere compliments
Thanks
Hugs
Our attention
A listening ear
A helping hand
Our time
Our love.

We need to remind ourselves often that love isn't real, honest, true love until it's given away. We give when we share in another's happiness or in his sorrow; at those times "just listening" is the very best gift we can offer.

Investing hugs, thanks, a helping hand, time, and love in the money-markets of our relationships can pay big dividends. No matter how the stock market fluctuates, dividends keep rolling in. No matter how financially rich or poor we are, by reinvesting those dividends we become wealthy in happiness and love for others as well as for ourselves. Finding ways to give of ourselves can be a rewarding adventure and will bring us greater returns than our investments.

H = Help

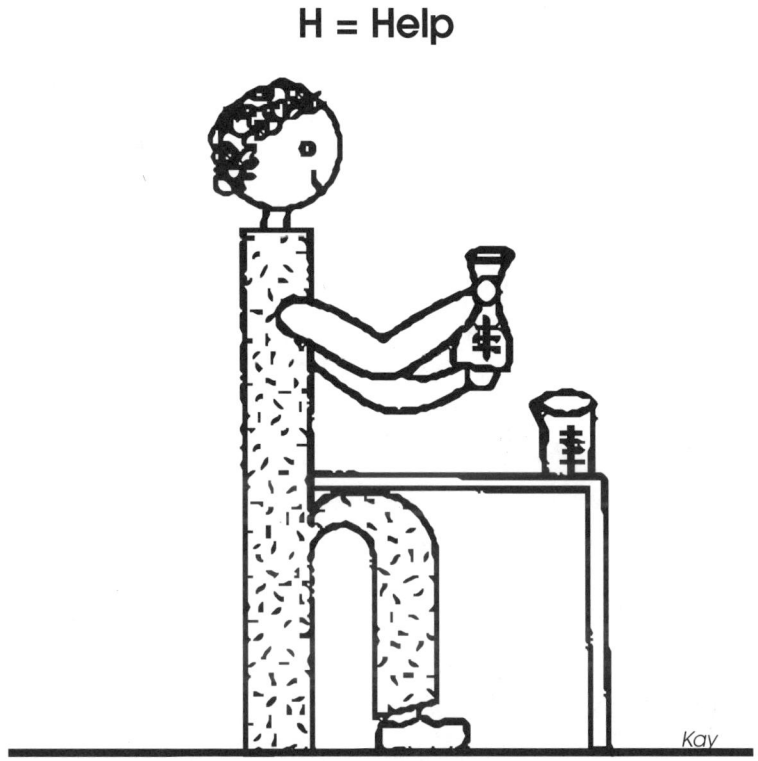

Kay

8. Can I Help You?

Leonore Hollander has done "a heap o' livin'" in her eighty-four years. Her mission in life seems to be to find a way to help wherever and whenever there is a need. She began to fulfill that mission when she was only eleven and took a bunch of violets to a classmate who was ill. She had forgotten the incident until many years later when she met her former classmate who reminded her, "It's the first time anyone ever did anything so nice for me."

Leonore's sentimental parents named her for the heroine in the opera Fidelio. The opera-Leonore helped to have her husband released from prison. Possibly having the same name has been the real-life Leonore's inspiration to help release people from their prisons, whatever those prisons might be.

After graduating from a public high school, Leonore was accepted at Bryn Mawr. When she finished at Bryn Mawr she received a scholarship to the University of Illinois where, in 1932, she earned her Ph.D. in Biochemistry. Leonore's father, a prominent chemist, encouraged her to follow in his professional footsteps.

On her first job at the Institute for Cancer Research in Philadelphia, Leonore met a young scientist from Prague who had come to the Institute to pursue studies on enzymes. They married after a year and when he returned to Prague, Leonore went with him. They found deep depression and political turbulence in the Europe of 1933.

Leonore helped her husband finish his Ph.D. in Prague. From there they moved to Heidelburg where they both worked for a chemist who had won a Nobel Prize. In Heidelburg they became keenly aware of anti-Semitism; Leonore's husband could not get an academic job because she is half Jewish. Because of the discrimination, Leonore and her husband moved to Darmstadt, Germany, where they lived for several years and where their three children were born.

It was in Darmstadt that the catastrophe of World War II overtook the family. Leonore recalls how terribly hungry they were; the agriculture and commerce industries in Germany had been destroyed and there was not enough food. They were deprived of more than food, however—Leonore had little contact with her family in the United States. Her only contact was through the Red Cross which was able to send one monthly message of twenty-five words to her family; her family could return an equally brief message.

By the end of the war, Leonore had been divorced and was anxious to bring her children back to America. When American servicemen arrived in Germany in the fall of 1945, they were under strict orders not to fraternize with the Germans. In spite of that order, Leonore talked an American officer into smuggling information to the Friends' Service Committee about the hardships suffered by displaced people in Europe. That information spurred the Service Committee to become active in the post-war relief program in devastated Europe.

In the spring of 1946, Leonore was able to get on the first ship that brought American civilians and many survivors of the infamous concentration camps to America. Her son, who was six, and her daughter, five, were the only small children on the ship; consequently, they received much attention and publicity.

On board ship, Leonore conducted classes in English conversation for her shipmates, most of whom were concentration camp survivors bearing tattoo numbers on their forearms. They appreciated Leonore's classes and the chance "for question-and-answer chat."

Leonore and her children lived with her parents in Philadelphia while she was seeking a job. She found it extremely difficult to get back into the job market: not only was she a woman seeking a position in a traditionally male field, but she had taken a ten-year hiatus from her career to bring up her children. She was finally hired as a Biochemist at St. Luke's Hospital in Bethlehem, Pennsylvania and stayed there for nine years.

When Leonore was a young student at Bryn Mawr, she became interested in the Society of Friends. Through that association she became acquainted with the Philadelphia Friends' Indian Committee. The Committee for Indian Rights was founded in 1794, the year the Iroquois were first seriously threatened with losing their land; the Friends' Committee was able to prevent that injustice. Leonore, always an activist for justice, joined the Committee in 1964 and served for twenty years.

Her involvement with Friends' international activities in the '60s brought Leonore in contact with an African student in the United States; his wife also wanted to study here. Leonore sponsored the wife so that she was able to receive her education. After completing their education, the couple returned to Kenya where he became a government official and she a Supervisor of Schools in Western Nairobi. Leonore is proud that she had a part in helping the young couple to become educated and return to Africa to educate others. She had the pleasure of visiting them in their home in Nairobi in 1971.

Leonore's home reflects her interest in Native Americans and in all things African. Her African treasures have a special place on the mantel; Native American dolls, wall hangings, and other Indian artifacts are prominently displayed.

Leonore made her first trip to California to visit her daughter in 1967; in 1984 she decided to make California her permanent home. The fact that she was 78 did not stop her from driving, with a companion, across the country from Pennsylvania to California.

A new Friends' retirement community was being

built in a city near where her daughter lived. Leonore "had been interested in the Friends' community from the time it was a gleam in somebody's eye." She chose, however, not to move into the community at that time, but she is closely associated with the activities there and will probably become a resident in the near future.

Leonore's desire to help has rubbed off on her family: her daughter is a midwife and an activist and her grandson is a "third-generation activist."

To this day, wherever Leonore sees a wrong, she wants to make it right. Her letters expressing her concerns are often published in the Letters to the Editor section of the local newspaper. She writes letters to her Congressmen and encourages others to do so. Leonore has a great affinity for the outdoors and serves on a Friends-in-Unity-with-Nature committee. Leonore insists, however, that she now stays out of most committees. "At 84," she says, "I think it is time for me to move aside and let younger people take over." Nevertheless, you can be sure Leonore will be there to help when she is needed.

H = Help

For every "helper" there must be a "helpee." Most of us believe it is better to be the helper than to be the one who receives help. This belief probably began in childhood when we first declared, "I can do it by myself!"

Independence, doing everything for oneself, is mistakenly seen as a strength, while dependence is considered weakness. Those concepts are not necessarily true—there is a time for both dependence and independence. There are times when we need to have the privilege of helping others, and there are times when others need to have the privilege of helping us.

It is important for a person of any age to know that it is O.K. to ask for help and to accept it without maintaining, "I *should* be able to do it myself." In the natural process of aging, our bodies lose some physical strength; our seeing and hearing capabilities become less acute. That is a fact of life and not one to make us feel less than a whole person. It becomes time for us to receive, to let others help us.

The roles of "helper" and "helpee" became very clear to me when my sister, a young 70-year-old, broke her shoulder and I became her helper. One day she came to me in tears because she could not open a child-proof bottle cap with her one good hand. She insisted, "It is because I am *old*." It took much persuasion to convince her that she could not have opened the same bottle with one hand when she was ten: *if* she was convinced—she may have pretended to be convinced to turn off my barrage of words.

Another time, my sister decided she could put on her blouse without my help in spite of having her arm in a sling. I was reluctant to give up my role of helper (and the satisfaction it was giving me) and insisted that she needed my assistance. She rejected my offer and proved she could do it herself. She was as proud as when, as a little girl, she tied her shoelaces for the first time. All of us need to have the satisfaction of doing for ourselves what we are able to do.

Besides physically helping others, there are other ways we can help. Some of us have financial resources to assist a grandchild or friend to get an education or to become established in business. Regardless of our physical or financial capabilities, we can encourage, we can be a friend, and we can listen,

Some seniors help others with their income tax forms; some of us let them help us. Some drive vans or buses to take those who no longer drive to the doctor or to buy groceries; still others deliver meals-on-wheels. Regardless of how old we are, we can help promote peace by being peaceful within ourselves and by living peacefully with our families and neighbors.

Whether it is our turn to be a "helper" or to be a "helpee," we must remember that one role is needed just as much as the other.

I = Interested And Interesting

9. A Rich And Wonderful Life

Deciding which interesting project to work on each day is Melba Garrett's biggest problem. She has many things "in the works." Although Melba officially retired eighteen years ago, she is still working to complete all of her projects.

Melba has a special interest in books: reading them, writing them, and compiling those written by others. She is assembling a book of unpublished scripts written by a friend who died leaving a wealth of material which Melba believes should be published. As a work of love, she is illustrating a book of Haiku verse written by her sister-in-law before she died.

There are even more books in Melba's future. The Organic Garden and Nutrition Club, which she joined soon after she retired, published a Newsletter with "wonderful articles." Melba has saved those articles and is binding them into a book.

The sermons delivered by the minister of the Unitarian Church which Melba attends are much too valuable to be lost; consequently, Melba has made it her special task to collect those sermons into yet another book.

When she can find a few extra hours between her other projects, Melba is writing her own book which she has titled *Homespun Yarns*. She chose the title for its special meaning which stems from her educational background and her love for reading, writing, and telling stories.

Melba was born in Centralia, Washington, in 1907 where, in her childhood, she was surrounded by her father's library. She was allowed to play with his books, stacking them, sorting them and rearranging them the way other little girls play with dolls; books were her companions.

Melba received her degree from University of Washington's School of Education where she majored in Home Economics, emphasizing Textiles and Clothing. As she taught Home Economics for fifteen years, she became aware of the shortage of resources available to teachers and decided to remedy the situation.

This meant returning to college to become credentialed as a school librarian, a challenge which she found both interesting and enjoyable. Melba speaks fondly of her thirteen years as Librarian for the San Mateo City School District in Northern California and her years in rural Mariposa County where the schools were often one or two rooms.

Melba had an interesting experience when she was still teaching. She was ill and had to spend several months in bed. One day, as she lay on her back looking at the ceiling, she saw in her mind a map of the world projected on a series of three equilateral triangles so that the round world would lie flat. When she regained her health and became active again, she drew the map just as she had envisioned it on the ceiling and produced it as a valuable resource for teachers to use in the classroom.

When Melba began to think about retirement, she decided that she should sample it for a year to determine if she would be happy away from her job. Her chance to sample it came when her nephew invited her to visit him and his family in Germany. They introduced her to the beauty of Germany, after which she traveled Europe alone by Eurail and knew that she was ready to retire.

Since she retired, Melba has renewed her spinning and weaving skills at a local junior college. Homespun Yarns is a natural product of her education, interests, and talents. Her knowledge of fabrics has prompted her to choose, for the front and back covers, a print reproducing the "whig rose" pattern of a favorite fabric.

According to Melba, she gets most of her ideas for writing when, "I have been lying at rest and allowing things to pop into my head. After a night's sleep I get up and sit down and write, write, write. So many of these things I write early in the morning." Melba shares those early-morning stories with an autobiographical writing class she attends. Many of her stories will be included in *Homespun Yarns* when she finds time, between her other projects, to organize and assemble them.

If Melba hadn't been a teacher and a librarian, she would have been an architect. Because of her interest in architecture, she helped design the sewing room for the local Senior Center, then she volunteered to organize and teach a sewing class. After nine years, she decided it was time to let someone else take over. She continued, however, to make her own clothes and to sew for children whose parents could not afford to buy their clothes.

Melba was one of the first residents in a new retirement community which opened in her city. Her bookmaking skills came in handy when she helped to collect and publish a souvenir booklet of residents' pioneer experiences to celebrate its fifth anniversary.

Melba owns a small home which she rents at a discount, usually to young families, because she believes it is important to help children get a good start in life. She has influenced and inspired many lives in her roles of teacher, librarian, sewing instructor, landlord, and friend.

After telling me about her life and experiences, Melba concluded, "It makes a very rich and wonderful life. I am rich in associates and friends and people who have touched my life. If I could write about each of them—oh, dear, the volumes I would have."

I = Interested And Interesting

To be interesting we must be interested. We must be interested in the world outside of ourselves—a world of people, of nature, of learning, and a world of ideas; interested in the past and the future as well as in the present.

We all have the potential for being interesting. Each life at birth is an empty book with blank pages; from that day until the day we die we fill those pages with our experiences. If it were possible to go back and reread those volumes, we would be amazed at the number and variety of people we have known, the places we have been, and the sights we have seen. We would remember the history we have lived, the books we have read, the feelings we have felt, and the ideas we have entertained. In the course of those years we have accumulated knowledge and experience and collected skills and wisdom that cannot be learned from books, but can only be acquired from life by living it.

When we contemplate the whole of our lives, the changes we have seen and experienced in even the last fifty years, we can only be curious about what the future holds for the next generation. In what kind of world will they live? What will space exploration mean for them? Will there be cures for today's baffling diseases? Will there finally be peace in the world? An end to prejudice? The future promises to be exciting.

Every person whose life story I have told in this book is interested and interesting. Each has a keen and lively awareness and is participating in life. Melba Garrett's bookmaking keeps her constantly busy and interested as she accumulates, sorts, organizes, writes, and draws. Each keeps interested in his or her own unique way. There are so many people to meet and so many things to do in this world that we need never be bored. We only need to choose from the rich banquet spread before us. We can look forward eagerly to each new day knowing there are new experiences to be added to our life stories.

J = Jam

Kay

10. Sing Along With Helen

Never too old to jam! What an unlikely description of a woman who has reached the age of 86! But it is the right word to describe Helen King. She is happiest when she and her music mates are "doing their thing" on their chosen instruments. Helen plays the acoustic piano; the others play an electric piano, an electric organ, and a banjo.

According to Helen, "My music is a gift which came through my mother's family. Mother loved music and had a piano." Helen's mother was determined that

Helen would become a musician and began giving her piano lessons when she was six. Her mother, like all good parents, insisted that Helen practice an hour a day; Helen, like all normal children, objected by using the familiar excuse, "I can't sit for an hour; my back hurts." Eventually Helen proved she was right—she did have a back problem and still has; however, it has not stopped her from enjoying many happy years at the piano.

Helen was born in Booneville, Indiana, where she lived until she was seventeen and moved with her family to Oklahoma. Helen remembers that they had no lights in their new home for the first two weeks, making it impossible for her to amuse herself by reading. To keep from being bored, Helen began playing the piano in the dark and learned that she didn't need to see the music to play. She tells it this way: "I discovered that I could play anything by ear, which is a great joy and very liberating and startling to others. After my unhappy lessons at the age of six, I never took formal lessons, nor practiced, nor tried to read music."

As a college coed Helen was the popular pianist at all of the dances. She enjoyed playing, "but it got tiresome being there and not being able to dance."

Helen received her B.A. in English at the University of Oklahoma. At that time she was intrigued with oil geology and worked for two years as an oil geologist. She returned to Indiana intending to get her Masters at the University; however, she changed her plans when she fell in love and chose the degree of MRS. instead of M.A.

Helen's MRS. led to motherhood. While she was searching for the "right" nursery school for her daughter, she met a woman who had trained at Columbia University and believed in the Montessori method of teaching. The two of them put their heads, their training, and their talents together and opened their own nursery school using Montessori methods and materials.

After World War II, Helen, with her husband and children, moved to Northern California where they bought a chicken ranch, a popular but not a profitable business at that time. To help make ends meet, Helen opened a nursery school which she describes as "a satisfying thing but not a gold mine."

When she had worked ten years as a struggling nursery school teacher, a friend asked her why she didn't get into the public school system where she could make more money. When Helen investigated, she learned that if she assumed a heavy class schedule for a few months, she would qualify to teach in public school. Although getting a teaching certificate demanded much time and hard work, Helen achieved her goal and a job was waiting for her.

Helen taught in the public school system for eight years before she retired; she was sixty-five. She and her husband wanted to travel and they did travel— far and wide; they began by circling the globe aboard a freighter. They enjoyed that trip so much they chose to visit Australia and New Zealand the same way.

After her husband died, Helen continued to travel by herself or with friends. She has visited Hawaii, South America, and the Caribbean. On one occasion, she and three friends spent four weeks in England, Wales, and Scotland. One of her happiest memories is that of a trip to Western Samoa to visit her daughter and son-in-law who were serving there as volunteers in the Peace Corps. Her most recent adventure was sailing on the Q.E.II through the Panama Canal and on to New York and Washington, D. C.

Helen lived on the ranch until she sold most of it to a developer and moved into a retirement center. She still owns the ranch house and is having the carriage house remodeled into a granny unit in which she plans to live someday.

Several years ago, a local artist, not well-known at the time, painted a picture of Helen's ranch house in exchange for an antique violin which she had inherited. Since that exchange, the artist has gained an enviable reputation and Helen is the proud owner of one of his early paintings.

Helen's apartment is filled with treasures of sentimental value. Among those treasures is a quilt made by a great-aunt while her husband was away fighting in the Civil War; every stitch was done by hand. An antique hall tree, refinished by Helen's husband, holds her hat collection, and wall-hangings display old lace pieces made by her mother.

Helen and her musical friends—they call their group Music Makers—"are all on the same age level; we all play without notes and we have a ball." The Music Makers were awarded a silver bowl by the Carnation Milk Co. for volunteering their time and talents to entertain at senior centers, convalescent hospitals and Golden Age groups.

Because she is able to play by ear, Helen is often called on to play for Sing-Alongs. She is rarely stumped by a request for a particular song; her playing is lively and soon everyone is caught up in the fun.

Helen is not sure she agrees with the policy of

"stimulating older people to be what they once were."
She believes that "aging is a normal and natural thing.
You have to listen to your body and adjust yourself to
it." She knows when she needs to rest and schedules
her activities around her rest time.

Many years have come and gone since the night
Helen realized she could play the piano in the dark,
a talent which has given her and countless others hours
of enjoyment. I can just see Helen sitting on her heav-
enly cloud jamming on her celestial piano instead of
gently plucking the strings of a celestial harp.

J = Jam

The word "jam" has several definitions, some
seem to contradict the others; some are restrictive
while others are non-restrictive. Those restrictive definitions are:

- to press into a close or tight position; to
  crowd; squeeze; wedge in.
- to become blocked, wedged, or fixed.

Those non-restrictive are:

- to play (a piece) in a freely improvised,
  swinging way; jazz up.
- jam session— a meeting of a group of
  musicians, especially jazz musicians, to
  play for their own enjoyment.

The non-restrictive definitions describe the feeling of Helen and her friends holding a jam session.
Their jamming is freedom of expression, spontaneity,
enjoyment, releasing their spirits. There is nothing
"blocked, wedged, or fixed" about their music; it is

free, liquid, and moving. It dances and leaps from their instruments. Bubbles of music fill the room. The musicians are so involved with their music that you know it is coming from deep inside them.

In our older years, many of us have more freedom than we have ever before experienced. We have raised our families and we have retired from the work-a-day world. We no longer worry about achieving fame or fortune. It is our time to "jam"—to express our freedom.

Many of us cannot play an instrument as Helen and her musical friends do, but we can express our freedom in other ways—we can laugh and we can be spontaneous in our expressions of pleasure and delight.

The Music Makers' jam sessions give each member the opportunity to express his own uniqueness. Just as each of the Music Makers is unique, so are we. It is mind-boggling to realize that never, since time began, has there ever been anyone exactly like me. In millions and billions of people, I am the only "me" and I am free to express "me" in my own unique way.

A jam session would not be a jam session without people sharing in expressing themselves. In the same way, we need others to share in the expression of our individuality. We can make beautiful music by ourselves, or express ourselves in another way, but it is more fun when we "make music" together. We can bounce feelings and ideas off each other. While we retain our individuality, we harmonize together.

What definition of "jam" do we want to accept? Do we want to be "pressed into a closed or tight position, crowded and squeezed . . . become blocked, wedged, or fixed," or do we want to "play in a freely improvised, swinging way"? How we choose to jam is our choice.

K = Keep Fit

Kay

11. Healthy In Body, Mind, And Spirit

Three parties were required to celebrate Reverend Albert Corpening's 90th birthday adequately, and he enjoyed all three of them. Those 90 years began in Banner Elk, North Carolina, on Thursday, November 9, 1899.

Reverend Corpening—known as Al to his friends—radiates an energy and physical fitness which makes it difficult to believe his true age; however, his fitness is no accident. He "grew up on a farm and ate lots of vegetables, potatoes, fruit and some meat." Milk and water were his regular beverages then and still are to this day.

Keeping fit is as important to Al today as it was in his youth. He has established a routine of daily exercise: besides walking, he does sitting-up exercises. "Those include everything one can do to exercise every muscle in the body." He includes exercising his eyes and is happy to say, "My glasses have not needed changing for over fifteen years."

Although he lived alone for many years after his wife died in 1985, after 57 years of marriage, Al continued to fix nutritious meals for himself. Al neither drinks nor smokes. He believes his physical strength hasn't changed much since he was forty or fifty. Al recently moved into a retirement home where he enjoys the luxury of three meals a day which he does not have to prepare nor does he have to wash the dishes.

When we learn how much energy Al burned up in his career years, and is still burning up, we have to agree that it is a good thing he has maintained his good health. After he graduated from high school Al earned several advanced degrees, including a Masters in Theology. He planned to get his Ph. D. at University of Chicago where he was admitted on a fellowship; unfortunately, he had "to drop out for lack of funds in those Depression years."

Al was ordained a Baptist minister when he was twenty-one. He held pastorates while he attended college and later when he taught in college; he was a full-time pastor for churches in Indiana and Illinois for many years. Even in retirement, Al continues to minister; he has completed seventeen interim pastorates since he "retired."

Al served as Chaplain in the Civilian Conservation Corps (CCC) for seven years, and in 1934 he was commissioned as a Chaplain in the U. S. Army Reserves; he served two years in the office of the Chief of Chaplains in Washington, D. C., and was Chaplain to the 12th Army Air Corps in Corsica and Italy. He retired from the active reserves at the age of 62.

Al may have celebrated his 90th birthday, but he hasn't slowed down much. In Franklin, Indiana, where Al lives, he teaches a Sunday School class at the First Baptist Church; he belongs to The Army and Navy Chaplains Association, The Reserve and Retired Officers Association, and the Chamber of Commerce. The Chamber of Commerce honored him as Senior Citizen of the year in 1984. Al has been an active member of Kiwanis for more than thirty years; he serves on the Spiritual Aims committee of the Franklin Kiwanis Club which, according to Al, "is very active and community minded."

Al's interest in research, in his younger years and today, is devoted to learning more about the Bible; he is presently researching the approximate date of the writing of Deuteronomy.

According to a friend who knows Al well, his interests increase as his years increase. His curiosity, added to his dedication to exercising and eating properly, help to keep Al young. He does not have time to count his wrinkles; he is too busy keeping himself fit, teaching, learning, and enjoying his family and friends.

K = Keep Fit

"74-year old woman climbs to top of Kilimanjaro."

"Eric de Reynier, 83, took up hang gliding when he was 72 and has ridden currents as high as 2,500 feet and as long as an hour."

"Hoppy Swarts, 70, won the Pacific Coast surfing championship for men 45 years and up in 1983."

"Ada Thomas, 73, started jogging after she retired. She now jogs five miles a day."

These are only a few of the stories from my Positive Aging scrapbook. Are these people just the lucky ones who have been blessed with good health and physical fitness? I don't think so. I believe they have chosen to work at keeping their bodies healthy. They have chosen to exercise, eat nutritiously, maintain a positive attitude, enjoy life, and leave the smoking to others.

The word "health" means the same as "whole"; the dictionary defines it as "the state of being sound in body, mind and soul." We have responsibility for keeping our once-in-a-lifetime body healthy; it is a treasure chest which holds the machinery for living and it is beyond price. We come into this world with a body which has to last us as long as we live; we had better keep it in tip-top condition. We cannot turn it in for a new one, although advances in medicine are making giant strides toward replacing certain body parts.

To a great extent, aging is in our minds. We can live a long time without getting old if we make up our minds to stay healthy and active. Some people believe that all old people are in poor health; that is not true. We can help to keep our bodies and minds healthy by being involved in the things that matter to us. It is important that we stimulate our minds as well as exercise our bodies. Health, fitness, and exercise go hand in hand.

Studies on the subject of exercise and the older

person have proved that tremendous benefits can be gained from a regular exercise program. Most of all, we should enjoy whatever form of exercise we choose—make it a game, not a dreary responsibility. If we enjoy swimming, dancing, or walking, we can get our exercise and have fun while doing it.

Al Corpening has chosen to keep himself fit by establishing a daily exercise routine. Besides walking, Al does sitting-up exercises for his body and research to keep his mind healthy. His faith and attitude keep his spirit well and healthy.

Al, as well as the woman who climbs mountains, the one who jogs five miles a day, and the men who hang-glide and surf, knows the importance of keeping fit. We, like they, can give good health priority in our lives. The treasure chest of our whole self is much too valuable to neglect.

L = Learn

Kay

12. Never Too Late To Learn

As the last notes of Handel's Piano Concerto faded away, the applause began. Bertha Klein had played a difficult concerto at her graduation ceremony. This was no ordinary graduation and Bertha was no ordinary graduate. Bertha, at the age of 92, was graduating from an Elderhostel program at St. Joseph's college, Hartford, Connecticut, in the summer of 1989.

Fifty men and women, sixty and older, had spent a week together, living in the dormitory, eating in the cafeteria, and attending classes, just as 750 young college students do from September to June.

All week Bertha had attended the mind-stretching classes in mathematics, architecture, and autobiographical writing. She was the first to ask probing questions and to offer information from her vast store of knowledge and experience. She expressed ideas and made observations convincing the rest of us that she was a bright and knowledgeable lady. She was physically agile, as well—when others rode the elevator, she walked up the stairs.

After spending that week with Bertha I knew she was a perfect role model for positive aging and I wanted to know what put that sparkle in her eye and how she became so wise. That was the beginning of a friendship which keeps letters flying between Connecticut and California.

Bertha was born in 1897 on a farm in Virginia. As was the custom, her first school was one room with one teacher. Her first day at school was a disaster! Life in her quiet family, with one younger sister, had not prepared her for the bedlam of loud, rough boys storming out for recess. She was so frightened that first day that she ran home crying and declared that she would never go back to school.

Bertha was blessed with a wise mother who decided to teach Bertha at home. "She got books from the Seventh Day Adventist's School System for not only reading, 'riting' and 'rithmetic', but also for history, geography, and chemistry. A teacher came to our house once or twice a week to get me started, but soon she said I had learned all I needed for one year and she was sure we would get along fine without her."

"Those were wonderful years," Bertha remembers. "I loved to learn, Mother loved to teach, and how lively and demonstratively she did it!" Bertha paints a vivid picture of the unique way her mother taught the subject of astronomy. She concludes, "I didn't think there was another child on earth who had such a loving and intelligent education."

When Bertha was eleven she moved with her parents and sister to Germany where her grandmother and other relatives lived. The girls attended a high school for girls and Bertha "had piano lessons off and on, when we could find a teacher who was not too expensive." When Bertha was in the upper grades she had the satisfaction and pleasure of tutoring some of the slower learners in the lower grades.

Bertha says about continuing her education: "It was my last, my 10th year in school, 1914, when Germany entered the War. Because some of our teachers had to enlist, our class could not complete its program, which would have been the equivalent of the first year in college. That bothered my vanity for many years. Instead of learning, we were knitting socks and mittens for the soldiers."

Bertha did manage to get more education by "taking lessons in bookkeeping, in sewing, in dressmaking." In 1919 she entered nursing school, received her license as a registered nurse in a year, and went into private nursing with the Nurses Registry of the Seventh Day Adventists. Because she had been trained to be a medical missionary and had her heart set on going to India, she was disappointed that Germany had no connections with India; the only country open to German missionaries was Africa and she did not want to go to Africa.

In 1924 Bertha married a German man who owned and managed a natural food store. They had one child, a son. She opened her own Vegetarian Restaurant in 1929 and ran it for thirteen years. She enjoyed that experience. "The restaurant brought me in touch with all kinds of health and spiritual organizations and interesting people." She had to give up her restaurant after America entered the War; she had divorced her German husband, making it unlawful for her, an American citizen, to run a business in Germany. Although she was offered German citizenship three times, she chose to return to America instead.

In 1946, Bertha returned to the United States where she supported herself and her son by working as a nurse, a career she continued until she was almost ninety.

Bertha, at 92, is still learning and, in turn, is teaching two students German, the language she spoke much of her life. She is also teaching English to the wives of Indonesian men who are in the United States attending college.

Bertha's letters are inspiring. In one she wrote: "We have had such beautiful autumn days. 'Oh, what a beautiful morning, oh, what a beautiful day! I have a wonderful feeling—everything's coming my way!' I just can't help singing that! Even a foggy, rainy morning has its charm. I wonder what Nature is hiding from me, busy at some mysterious doings!"

Bertha is wise with a wisdom that comes from 92+ years of living, keeping an open mind, being curious, being willing to learn and to teach, and hours and years of reading. Bertha's words reflect her wisdom and philosophy: "Learning or studying something new is really rejuvenating, I have found; or *doing* something new. The sense of adventure makes me feel like a child again."

"It has occurred to me that it is very important to live without stress, in order to stay healthy. Therefore my morning prayer contains the plea—'*You* design the day for me.' Now, when my plans are thwarted, I don't get frustrated, I ask myself, 'What are God's plans today?' And, lo and behold, the day turns out perfectly. Of course, that is an old wisdom—'bouncing with the bumps' they call it."

"I used to fear the thought of growing old, but I now become more and more grateful for all the beauties and blessings of life. I am looking forward to the incoming 'Golden Age' and hope to be around to enjoy it!"

Bertha didn't conclude her education when she graduated from Elderhostel; less than a month later she attended a Senior Summer Camp at Camp Connri in Connecticut. The Hartford *Courant* published a picture of Bertha working a crossword puzzle during the week she spent at camp. It reported that she, at 92, was the oldest person at the camp and quotes her as saying, "It's like gate No. 2 to heaven."

L = Learn

"Lots of Gray Hair Under Those Caps" was the headline of the local paper on June 1, 1991. The caps were graduation caps and the gray hair belonged to the older graduates. The oldest graduate from the local college that day was 74 and the youngest was 21. It is not unusual today to have gray heads receiving their diplomas and it will be even more common in the years ahead because more and more older people are returning to the classroom.

In my scrapbook are wonderful stories of people who have returned to high school or college many years past the traditional school age. In May 1990, a 97-year-old woman in Lowell, Ma., received her high school diploma as valedictorian for a class of nursing home residents. She quit school when she was seventeen and returned to classes after an absence of eighty years. According to her, "It is uplifting and inspiring to work toward this goal because it keeps your mind alert and aware of community and world affairs."

A Maryland woman returned to school at eighty and received her bachelor's degree from the University of Maryland when she was 85. She maintained a 3.69 grade point average and earned membership in Phi Beta Kappa. She says she did it because she didn't want to be a time-waster.

Brain research has shown that development and growth of the brain goes on into old age if a person exercises his brain by studying and being open to new experiences. A challenged brain simply never quits learning.

Learning doesn't have to take place only in the classroom; every experience is its own classroom. Because we learn from others and they learn from us, we are all teachers as well as students. Our challenge is to be sure that the lessons others learn from us are the best we can teach. Older people are natural teachers out of their years of experience.

*Elderhostel** has become a popular way for the no-

---

* *Elderhostel* catalogs can be found in libraries and on college campuses. The address for more information is: *Elderhostel*, 75 Federal Street, Boston, MA 02110.

longer-young to combine travel and fun with learning. According to the *Elderhostel* Catalog, "Elderhostel is an educational program for older adults who want to continue to expand their horizons and to develop new interests and enthusiasms . . . *Elderhostel* is for older citizens on the move, not just in terms of travel, but in terms of intellectual activity as well."

If used properly, television can be a valuable source for learning. Experts in every field come into our homes at the touch of a button. Never have we had so much knowledge available from so many sources. All that is required of us is an open, curious, and receptive mind.

Learning is more than becoming an expert on facts and figures. We can learn to know and understand ourselves and why we are who we are. We can learn to listen to our inner voice and how not to be a puppet manipulated by others. Continuing to learn, no matter how old we are, makes us more interesting; it helps us to understand our world and the people in it; it makes our lives richer. Our challenge is to never stop learning.

M = Mentally Alert

Kay

13. Inspired By Claude Monet

When I arrived at the Frey home to learn about Hans Frey's life, he met me at the door with blue paint on his hands. He had been busy in his studio painting a picture on a 6"x 6" ceramic tile.

Stepping into the Frey home is like walking into an art gallery. The eye is quickly drawn to an age-darkened picture of a young man, a painting made many years ago by an Austrian artist before he became famous. According to Hans, that painting would be priceless in Austria today. In contrast to the dark colors in the old painting are the fresh, bright colors of Hans' watercolor pictures and ceramic tiles.

Hans, the artist, was "inspired by Claude Monet who painted some of his masterpieces when he was old." Hans, at 95, paints every day, still producing his masterpieces.

Hans and Anna Frey, married 56 years ago, typify the true meaning of the marriage vows: "two becoming one." Although I came to hear Hans' story, he quickly informed me that I should be talking to Anna instead. He gives her the credit for what he is able to do. He insists, "She takes care of me and encourages me." It was plain to see that he spoke the truth—she is proud of him and of his artistic accomplishments.

Hans was born in Vienna into a well-to-do family which was able to give him and his brother many privileges. His parents hired a young man to teach the boys; the young teacher took them on hikes where he taught them to sketch objects and landscapes. Later Hans had other good teachers who inspired him to continue to sketch and paint, a hobby he has enjoyed all of his life.

Anna was also born in Vienna. She and Hans met at the home of a mutual friend. About their meeting, Anna maintains, "It was destiny."

In Vienna Hans was a Doctor of Law and worked as Executive Secretary for a large insurance company; he was the personnel manager and managed the company's building. He held that job for nineteen years until Hitler came into power and they had to flee. Hans declares that they were lucky not to be arrested and imprisoned in a concentration camp.

When they fled from their country, Hans and Anna

had been married four years and had no children. Hans' brother, with two small daughters, fled at the same time. The Frey family left Vienna by train in January 1939; they went to England where they lived until November, then sailed to the United States to begin new lives and establish new careers.

Hans and Anna's first home in America was in Chicago where he contributed to the publication of a weekly column transcribed from medical papers written by physicians. At one time he was supervisor of the department and had people from several countries working with him.

Anna helped Hans to get established by working as a milliner and a teacher of crafts. Then it was Anna's turn to go back to school. She earned her degree in Social Work when she was 48 and worked with older people at the first senior center in Chicago. She continued to work as a social worker until she retired.

In America the Freys missed the mountains where they had spent many hours hiking and camping; the flat plains of the Midwest were nothing like the Austrian Alps. They were delighted when they discovered the Rocky Mountains in their new country.

Hans and Anna have returned to Austria seven times. Their last trip was made in 1982 when Anna attended a conference on Aging while Hans hiked in his beloved Alps.

Friends House, a retirement community in Northern California, became the Frey's home when it was opened to its first residents. Their niece, who was on the Board of Friends House, recommended that they move there and they are glad they took her advice.

Although Hans had painted in oils most of his life,

he had given up oils by the time they moved into their new home. When a watercolor class was started, Anna encouraged Hans to go "and so I went. I do only flowers in this class." Each October the artists exhibit and sell their paintings to benefit Friends House. Hans sold several of his art works last year and plans to exhibit again.

I had heard about Hans' artistic ability even before I met him. A friend of his gave me a small notepaper which he had decorated with dried flowers, and a photograph of one of his watercolors. Neighbors and friends collect their small, colorful flowers for Hans who presses and dries them so that they retain their lovely colors.

Today Hans does most of his painting on ceramic tiles. His subjects are varied: flowers, landscapes, and his home in Vienna, all in pure and bright colors. On one tile he has reproduced a famous artist's painting so exactly that it is difficult to tell that it is a copy.

Anna and Hans are quite different in personalities. She is interested in people and enjoys socializing at Friends House, while Hans prefers quiet time alone to paint and read. A friend who lives in Germany supplies him with books written in German.

The nieces, who were small children when they left Vienna, live nearby and "are taking loving care of us." The nieces took them on vacation to see Mt. Shasta and are planning a trip to King's Canyon to enjoy the redwoods.

Besides producing masterpieces, Hans is a volunteer in the Friends House Library.

A conversation with Hans and Anna is stimulating; they are both articulate, interesting, and mentally active. Hans mentioned how grateful they are to be able to pursue their interests and to travel to the mountains even though they no longer hike. In Hans' opinion, "there is too much fuss being made about old age, too many studies and too much research. I believe that old age is a natural part of life and should be treated that way."

The Freys are a happy couple in their California home. In Hans' words, 'When I sit here and see the flowers and the humming birds, it makes me very happy and satisfied. It is so beautiful and I enjoy it."

M = Mentally Alert

It is easy to recognize someone who is mentally alert. That person has a sparkle in his eye and an air of self-confidence. His whole bearing declares, "I am a worthwhile person and I have a purpose." He is a participant in life, looking forward to each new experience convinced that it will add to his well-being and give him an opportunity to learn.

The old adage "The proof is in the pudding" seems to be the best argument for mental alertness in people of any age. In my scrapbook are stories of older people who continue to do mental gymnastics. Those stories are all the proof I need that we are never too old to be mentally alert.

When I reread those stories, I am thrilled at the wisdom and accomplishments of people who are no longer young. One story is that of a woman who won the Nobel Prize for Medicine when she was seventy-seven. She is still, several years later, actively working in her field. Another is the story of a man who retired from a scientific research company—"under protest"—when he was seventy-seven. He "refused to be cast into an ashcan, with so much to learn and do in a world of teeming activity." He and his wife founded an institute for continuous learning on a university campus. The institute conducts study groups in disciplines ranging from archeology to zoology and features peer teaching by retired professionals.

"Author proves it's never too late" is a column headline in the Santa Rosa, California, *Press Democrat* of November 28, 1989. The author referred to is Harriet Doerr who wrote the best-selling novel, *Stones for Ibarra*. According to the article, the author "went back to college when she was sixty-seven, began writing and published her first novel when she was seventy-four."

The men and women in these stories are no different from you and me except that they may have been exercising their mental faculties more than we have. We can exercise our brains by using them in a variety of ways by:

- Taking classes, even by correspondence or television if we are unable to get out;

- Working crossword and other mind-expanding puzzles;

- Reading books and articles that make us think;

- Looking up the meanings of unfamiliar words and storing them in our memory banks;

- Writing a journal;

- Making it a habit to learn something new every day.

According to Dr. Frank S. Caprio in his book *Add Life to Your Years*, "Any mental task which you could perform capably at twenty or thirty-five, you can still do equally well at sixty, seventy, or very likely at an even greater age." He disagrees with the myth that all old people lose their mental agility. Dr. Caprio further states, "You need not grow old mentally, for the way you live your lives depends upon the way you think about yourself . . . The human mind matures, but it does not age, after the manner of our other organs."[1]

Recent research shows that age does not damage mental abilities as much as one believed, and in some areas we actually gain mental agility by learning to compensate through experience for much of what we might lose.

I found these encouraging words at an Elderhostel I attended:

> Whether you are 35 or 85, you no more need to look forward to senility than you do to heart disease or lung cancer. The healthy brain of an active adult is one of the most resilient organs Mother Nature has given us.
>
> The overall thinking skills of a 55-year-old are almost always markedly superior to those of a 25 year-old.

If we are not already doing mental gymnastics, today is the time to begin by collecting stories about older people who are keeping their minds active and alert. This book is a good place to begin. If these twenty-six people can remain mentally alert so can we.

---

1 Caprio, Dr. Frank S. Caprio, *Add Life to Your Years*, The Citadel Press, Secaucus, N. Y., 1975.

Kay

14. A *Century Of Living*

Goldie Barclay was 100 on March 22, 1991. Her special birthday did not slip by unnoticed; her friends at the retirement home had a party to celebrate the momentous occasion. They didn't try to put 100 candles on her cake—only sixteen and one to grow on. Goldie entertained her guests by reciting a poem she had written:

My Birthday

I noticed just the other day
  My friends are growing older
  In a gracious kind of way.
But not me—on me, it's showing.

> But what bothers me
>> And makes me shiver in my sandals
> Is when my birthday cake comes around
>> And I can't see the cake for the candles!

Goldie was born in Mason County, Illinois, where she lived with her parents, three brothers and two sisters most of her growing-up years. She met and married her "special" young man. During World War II Goldie and her husband worked in the aircraft industry. Following the war she was employed for ten years as a tailor in the women's suit department of a large retail store.

After her husband's death in 1959 Goldie shared her home for several years with an unmarried brother. When he died she decided that it was time to move to California where she could be near her son and his family. The warmer climate also appealed to Goldie. She bought a home north of San Francisco and lived there until she moved into the retirement home where she lives today.

Goldie has been a writer since she was young. She had never kept anything she wrote until her daughter-in-law "got after me when her boys (Goldie's two grandsons) were growing up. She caused me to save some things for them." Not long ago, Goldie collected many of those "things" into a book for her grandsons.

Until recently Goldie attended a writing class every week. She would still be attending if the class had not disbanded. In 1981 a friend typed, and copied on a copy machine, a small collection of Goldie's poems as a gift for her friends. She calls this little book *Facts and Fantasies*. This poem from that collection reflects her wit and imagination:

Stylish Mother

The day Mom came from the beauty shop
We didn't hardly know her,
Her hair was piled high up, on top
Like Jimmy's poodle's fur.

Pop took one look, "What's that," says he
"A nest for homeless mice?"
"New style," says Mom. "Go have your fun
We girls all think it's nice."

She turned her head this way and that,
Started feeding baby brother,
He yelled and kicked and bawled and squealed;
He didn't know our mother.

"Sh! Sh! Come to Daddy; Daddy's little baby,
That's your mother, see the pretty lady?"
Then Mama's face got red as red;
Her lips got pinched and tight;
And me, I sat just awful still;
I thought I'd see a fight!

But Mom just smiled, "My hair's in style
That way it's going to stay.
Seems you don't like my hair on top;
Well, look the other way."
"Ho, ho, ho," says Pop. "My dear,
    It's only fair,
I won't shave off one single beard
'Til you let down that hair!"

One of the many myths about aging is that all old
people are forgetful. That is not true about Goldie.

When she recites a poem she wrote fifty or more years ago, you can almost see the wheels of her mind turning. She may grope for a word momentarily, but she always finds it and continues to the end of the poem no matter how long it is. Each of her poems is her favorite. I love her honesty and candor when she recites or reads a poem—her eyes twinkle and she says, "Isn't that cute? I like that."

Music has been Goldie's lifelong pleasure. She was fortunate, she says, to attend schools that offered fine music classes. "From the sixth grade through high school we did advanced chorus work." She taught herself to play the family organ "by using the organ book"; later she had a few piano lessons — "maybe six months, not long." One of her early pleasures was "taking songs and changing them to suit myself."

Goldie's love for music has greatly influenced her family. She started her son "in the music business" and he went on to teach voice at a high school. Goldie speaks fondly of a musical daughter-in-law who, for twenty-eight years, accompanied a county chorus. It is no accident that Goldie's two grandsons are deeply involved in the music field—they inherited their mother's, father's, grandmother's, and great-grandmother's talents and love for music. One grandson is a concert pianist in Brooklyn; he also teaches in a college preparing music students for public performance. Goldie's second grandson is employed by a well-known music company; he teaches and is responsible for insuring the quality of the stringed instruments.

Goldie expresses a strong faith in God in a poem she wrote a few days after her husband's death.

Quiet Blessing

I was all alone that holy day;
I heard the church chimes sing,
And lifted my heart and soul to where
The thoughts of earth no longer cling
    To daily routine,
But to where saints and angels
Their praises sing.

I sat quiet, quick to hear
The pulse of God; I felt Him near.
No thought of worry or work or stress;
I sat alone,
    And I was blessed.

Although she uses a walker outside of her apartment, Goldie gets around her own place without help. She walks to the dining room for her meals and attends various activities with the other residents. She likes to go shopping.

Goldie describes herself as a person with the ability to adjust to changing situations. In the course of her 100 years she has been challenged many times to adjust—she has lost her husband, son, daughter-in-law, other family members, and dear friends. However, as long as she can write, enjoy music, friends and her grandsons, her life will continue to be full.

Our Earth

Is our earth just like a yo-yo—
Controlled by God's great hand,
That keeps it spinning, spinning,
To hold the sea and land?

And does He keep it spinning
To give us night and day
And never, never, ever
Lets it spin astray?

But keeps it spinning, rolling
Around its yearly course
To give us the four seasons
The east, west, south, and north?

Yes, it is just like a yo-yo
Spinning in the universe,
God's special planet made for man,
His yo-yo—we call Earth.

Two Worlds

Two little fish went out for a swim,
We'll call one Jack, the other one Jim.
Said Jack, "Those creatures up there on the sand,
Have no scales on their skin
And they don't swim;
What a strange world they live in."

But God made the fish to live in the sea
And God made the land for you and for me.
The fish for the sea, and the sand where boys play.
"Thank you, God. We like it that way."

To A Neighbor

He didn't fly an aeroplane
Nor construct a waterfall;
He didn't guide a radar beam
Or climb a mountain wall.

But of all the little things he did,
There really can be no end,
Because he's kept so busy
Just being a "good friend."

Goldie Barclay

N = Never Too Old

No one expects a 100-year-old to run in a marathon or to climb Mt. Everest. Our bodies age—a natural order of life. Our bodies have a built-in time schedule which operates from birth to death.

Our genes, at birth, are programmed to make our bodies grow, while they are programmed in old age to slow our bodies to prepare us for the end of life. This is biologically perfect.

In our young culture we tend not to accept old age as a perfectly natural part of life. We want to stop the process of aging at some year that we have chosen as ideal—possibly 16 or 21—or even 40, 65, or 85. The older years are often the most meaningful; they can be years of rich discovery.

Agism, like racism, is a blight on our society. Maggie Kuhn, founder of Gray Panthers, defines agism as "the notion that people become inferior because they have lived a specified number of years." She continues, "Old age is not a disease. It is strength and sur-vivorship, a triumph over all kinds of vicissitudes . . . Old age is also a time of great fulfillment—personal fulfillment, when all the loose ends of life can be gath-ered together. . . . I regard my wrinkles as badges of distinction—I've worked hard for them."[1]

Wise people are writing and speaking today in defense of old age. We learn that we can have a "pride of age." We need not apologize; we can be proud of the years we have lived.

The popular author, Leo Buscaglia, says about old age, "When we see reflected in a furrowed and lined face simply a lifetime that is used up, nothing more, we disregard a lifetime of accumulated wisdom. We fail to appreciate the imprint of time and the rich tapestry of experiences that is reflected in it. Think what a magnificent storehouse of memories are con-tained in a full life—the moments of passion, of con-tentment, of despair, of joy—things that the most sophisticated computer could never retain in its most complicated program."[2]

It is time for us former-young to put on our armor and battle the myths of aging. It is time for us to change our vision; only through our acceptance of whatever age we are, can we convince others.

Maggie Kuhn put on her armor several years ago. "She embodies a new philosophy of living whole

---

1 Porcino, Jane, Ph.D. *Growing Older Getting Better, A Handbook for Women in the Second Half of Life.* Addison-Wesley Publishng Company, Reading, MA, 1983. Foreword by Maggie Kuhn.

2 Buscaglia, Leo. *Bus 9 to Paradise.* William Morrow and Co., Inc., New York, NY, 1986.

when old. She is not asking everyone to try looking or acting younger; rather she is asking all to act their age as persons concerned for justice, confident of wisdom, open to self-discovery, ready to risk self-direction." She advocates "that we have been wrongly taught that old is a condition of loss, a time to quit, a mandate to withdraw. Can we demonstrate that old age is not a defeat, but a victory, not a punishment, but a privilege?"[3]

The story of 100-year-old Goldie Barclay is our answer to battling the myths of aging. She remains open to learning, enjoying and experiencing. She knows she has not become inferior because she has lived a century; the wisdom she has gained in that century is reflected in her poems and in her life.

---

3 Hessel, Dieter. *Maggie Kuhn on Aging*. Quoted from Alex Comfort's A *Good Age*.

O = Overcome

Kay

15. Giving As Well As Receiving

"I believe I fell in love with my doctor. He had to be away on sick leave once and I was so happy when he got back." To know the real importance of those words you need to know that the speaker, Mary Hartzog, is dependent on her doctor as few people are dependent on a doctor.

Mary has multiple sclerosis and is completely bed-ridden; she cannot leave her hospital bed even to sit in a wheelchair. Visiting Mary in her small apartment is a joy everyone should experience—she is cheerful, grateful, busy, understanding, and interested in what is going on in the world. She told me, "I like to help people however I can. The woman who comes in to assist me every morning was having a difficult time financially and I was able to advise her about ways to get her utility bills reduced. I've lived on a tight budget for a long time and I've learned ways to save."

Mary spends most of each day and every night by herself, but she insists she is not lonely and is not afraid. She has her telephone within easy reach so that she can call a young man who lives in the apartment next to her and he can be by her side in a few minutes.

I asked Mary how she was able to overcome loneliness and fear of being alone and she told me that simply having a caring person nearby whom she can call if she needs him keeps her from being afraid. She insures herself against loneliness by enjoying her T.V., radio, cassette tapes of her favorite saxophone player, books, and crossword puzzles. She visits her family and friends by telephone.

Mary became ill almost thirty years ago when she was a single mother with two small sons to raise. She is now sixty-seven. Mary admits that one of the first obstacles she faced when she was diagnosed as having multiple sclerosis was that of depression. She states honestly that it is very difficult to face the horror of learning that you are "stuck in bed" and can't do anything for yourself. Through the friendship and counsel of a young doctor whom she met soon after she was diagnosed, she was able to accept the terrible truth. She believes that a person who first receives the sentence of devastating chronic illness should have access to psychological counseling; it is too big a burden to carry alone. "At first it's such a shock. Becoming an invalid is tough. You become used to it after awhile, but you have fits of depression at first."

Since Mary has overcome her initial period of depression, she makes it very clear that she doesn't want anyone to analyze her or try to "cheer me up." "Nothing depresses me now," she says, "except sad movies; especially movies of sick children. I cry when I see those."

Mary is finally able to handle her anger at people who treat her as if she had a disease. "I've had people treat me as if I had something that was catching. They wouldn't come near me." Her advice to such people is, "Talk to the bedridden person; let them know that they are alive and can talk as well as the next person. Whatever I have is not going to rub off on you."

Going shopping used to be one of Mary's greatest pleasures. Although she is no longer able to go to the stores, she remains a careful shopper by reading the papers to find the best bargains, then she sends her helpers to buy the groceries, providing them with a list and coupons she has cut from the weekly ads.

Mary has a delightful sense of humor and enjoys teasing the people who work for her. She has a fantasy solution for overcoming the shortage of quarters to feed the washer and dryer at the apartment washroom—that solution is installing a "quarter tree next to my bed."

Mary is a care-giver as well as a care-receiver. Her care-giving goes to her closest companions, three beautiful blue and green parakeets, one noisy yellow canary and two "quiet" (Mary's words) goldfish. The canary complains loudly when the television is turned off, so Mary keeps it turned on for him even when she is busy working crossword puzzles or reading.

Just because Mary is not able to get out of bed does not mean she is not head of her house and queen of her domain. A helper, Diane, comes in every morning to get Mary's breakfast and get her ready for the day. Diane fixes Mary's dinner which she leaves with water and other things Mary might need, on a bedside table so that Mary can manage the rest of the day by herself. Her lunch is delivered by a volunteer from the Senior Nutrition Home Delivered Meals Program. On the weekend, a second home-helper comes in to clean for her and change her bed. Mary is determined that her helpers clean the window sills and in the corners even though she cannot inspect them. She kept a clean house when she could do it herself and insists on having a clean house now.

Mary lives in a downstairs apartment; she keeps her door open when it is warm enough, so that she can keep in touch with the outside world. As her neighbors pass her door to reach their apartments they call a cheery "Hi" or stop by to talk. Mary's two sons and two granddaughters come to visit her when they have time; when they are too busy to come by, they keep in touch by telephone.

The doctor whom Mary loves is a very important part of her life. She looks forward to his visits because he brings the outside world into her limited living space. He only comes every two months because, according to Mary, "other than multiple sclerosis, I don't have anything wrong with me." When he comes they have a chance to talk about anything and everything. He keeps her abreast of what is new in the study of multiple sclerosis as well as sharing with her thoughts about "music, today's kids, old people, books, anything that comes into our minds." She has great faith in her doctor and would feel free to call him if she needed him.

Mary is an inspiration. At sixty-seven, she has faced and overcome more problems than most of us have by the time we have reached our 80s and 90s.

O = Overcome

Overcome, in my opinion, means courage, determination, persistence, and positive attitude. You will not find those definitions in the dictionary, but they should be there just before, "to get the better of; to conquer; to gain superiority over; to win."

Many people overcome seemingly insurmountable obstacles and impossible situations. In the process, they often shed tears and become depressed, but courage and determination enable them to win. Some accept their challenges as opportunities to become wiser and stronger; others declare, "It isn't my fault; it's not fair" and do nothing to help themselves.

Public libraries have shelves lined with autobiographies and biographies telling fascinating and inspiring stories of overcoming. Some tell of succeeding in spite of physical impairments; others are stories of triumph over imprisonment, mental illness, poverty, and prejudice.

We, who are seniors today, have more help with meeting our challenges than any previous generation; there is new public awareness of the needs of seniors. A variety of agencies offer services to the home bound;

others provide for those who are mobile and active. Home delivered meals are life savers for people who cannot fix their own; Volunteer Wheels allow those who no longer drive to get to their doctors and to buy groceries.

Our most famous role model for overcoming is Helen Keller. She succeeded in spite of being blind and deaf, not by eliminating those handicaps, but by accepting them and learning how to live fully in spite of them. Each person must decide for himself—Will I be a victim or will I be an overcomer? Those who choose not to give in to hardships can find happiness and be an inspiration to others.

Mary Hartzog, Helen Keller, and thousands of others, remind us that it is possible to overcome, no matter how tough the problem. It is something we have to do for ourselves, and no one says it is easy!

P = Play

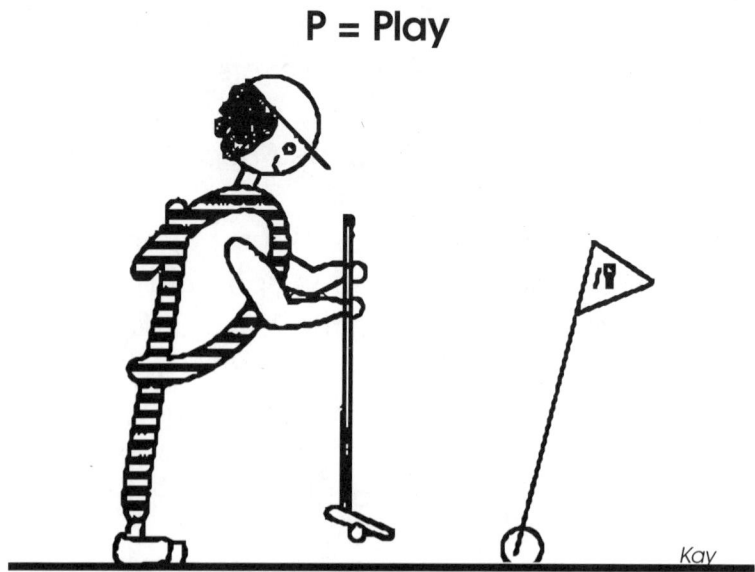

Kay

16. The Prime Year —The Big "80"!

Obviously, no one has told Myrle Cooper that it is O.K. to slow down and smell the roses when you reach eighty. She is still going full tilt just as she did when she was twenty. In high school Myrle was active in sports; in college she played Bridge besides keeping up with her studies; in marriage she and her husband enjoyed dancing and socializing. Fifteen years ago she learned to play golf which she does with the same vigor and enthusiasm she had for her earlier activities.

At the same time she was keeping a home and raising two sons, Myrle attended college classes and received a California Teaching Certificate allowing her to teach Adult Education Classes in Dressmaking, Tailoring and Wardrobe Planning. She continued taking classes and conducting workshops when she was a full-time teacher. Myrle was popular; anyone hoping to get into one of her classes had to register early.

Myrle's family has always come first in her life. When the boys were small, the family took sight-seeing trips; they camped and hiked in National Parks. She encouraged her sons in all of their activities: Demolay, Scouting and sports; she furnished transportation and refreshments and was always there for them.

Myrle gained a keen appreciation for music when she learned to play clarinet and piano in high school. When she retired from teaching, she bought an electric organ and spends many happy hours playing old and new songs. She seldom misses a Community Concert or a local theater production.

Life has dealt Myrle some staggering blows. Their retirement plans ended when her husband died suddenly after they had been married thirty years. She gives her faith in God and the support of her family and friends credit for helping her through that difficult time. In her words, "Memories, love in our marriage, raising two sons, seeing the older one through college before my husband's death, were the guiding lights to know I must go on—fortunately, the enjoyment of my teaching, too, was my salvation."

Tragedy visited Myrle a second time. Eight years after her husband's death, her older son was killed in a tragic accident, leaving his young wife and two small sons. Again, Myrle credits her faith and her work for getting her through that terrible time. Her younger son and she have been each other's strength.

Myrle has traveled extensively; she has visited Hawaii, Taiwan, Singapore, Bangkok, Hong Kong, and

Japan. She enjoyed a Caribbean cruise through the Panama Canal, and joined a Fashion Tour to London and Paris, as well as an Elderhostel to Scotland, England and Ireland.

Sandwiched in between Myrle's other activities, she has found time to teach a Sunday School class, volunteer in a hospital, be active in an Adult Education Association, and work three summers, after she retired, in a gift shop at a resort in the Canadian Rockies.

After thirty-two years of teaching, Myrle reluctantly decided to retire. It wasn't an easy decision to make because she loved teaching. She has not exactly retired, however; she is still deeply involved in college life—she works with registration and in the bookstore at a college near her home. She maintains that working at the college has contributed to "making my retirement rewarding and enjoyable, thanks also to my good health, good food, and lots of exercise."

Myrle calls this year—"The Prime Year!—The Big '80'!" With plans for more activities including one grandson's graduation from high school, and "looking ahead to the oldest grandson graduating from University next year." She adds, "Couldn't miss the only granddaughter's high school graduation." Myrle and her four grandchildren share a special relationship.

Besides being rich in family, Myrle is rich in friendships and you can be sure her Prime Year!—The Big '80'! will be just as busy as the past seventy-nine have been. Myrle is a shining example of aging positively.

P = Play

"All work and no play makes Jack a dull boy." That familiar proverb would be just as true if we were to reverse the words—"All play and no work makes Jack a dull boy." Both worktime and playtime are essential to a balanced, fulfilled life. Even in retirement, we have work to do: we must work at keeping our minds active, our muscles in shape, our bodies healthy, and our souls nourished.

We each have our own definitions for "play" and for "work." My definition for play may be your definition for work. My definition includes recreating, renewing, relaxing, enjoying, sharing, appreciating, cooperating, laughing, and loving. A football player's definition for play would include making a touchdown which would be my definition for work—very hard work.

Just as we grow from a child to an adult, our ideas of the meaning of play grow too. As an adult we may not care to sit on the floor to play jacks or hit a home run on the local ball diamond; however, we can continue to feel the deep satisfaction and enjoyment of participating and sharing in other ways.

There are a thousand ways to play; some are boisterous, active, and noisy; others are sedentary and quiet. When we play we can:

- Compete or cooperate
- Participate or act alone
- Swing the rope or jump
- Entertain or be entertained
- Perform or watch
- Run or sit
- Throw or catch

Today's elders have more time to play than those of any previous generation; we live longer and those added years give us extra time to use in a way we choose. We can do absolutely nothing and be bored, or we can find rewarding activities and be happy.

Creative people find creative ways to use their leisure. A group of men and women in my city get together once a week to have "Fun After 50." Some members of the group have formed the Kitchen Kut-Ups band; they play kazoos, keyboards, drums, and horns. In addition to playing for their own amusement, they perform once a year for the public. The weekly get-together is play and the annual Razzle-Dazzle combines play and work, both fulfilling and fun.

Some of us are not physically able or motivated to participate in a Kitchen-Kut-Ups group, but we can still play in our own way. The bedridden or wheelchair-bound person need not be denied the opportunity to take part in the playing side of life. I have a bedridden friend who knows how to play; she is an avid crossword puzzler; she keeps her dictionary within easy reach and spends hours increasing her vocabulary, keeping her mind keen, and experiencing the pleasure of filling every blank with the correct letter. Although she cannot dance or hike, she has found other ways to celebrate life.

Reading to a small child or sharing meals and memories with old friends—or new—are activities we might choose for recreation. Writing our autobiography, or reading, or collecting funny stories. Ask yourself, "Do I spend enough time at play?" If your physical body, your mental self, or your soul needs revitalizing, make a list of some ways you might play. Just making the list can be fun. Dig up some dreams that you filed away and forgot many years ago; decide to pursue those dreams in a quiet way in your new leisure; this may be the perfect time to "play" them into reality.

Q = Quality

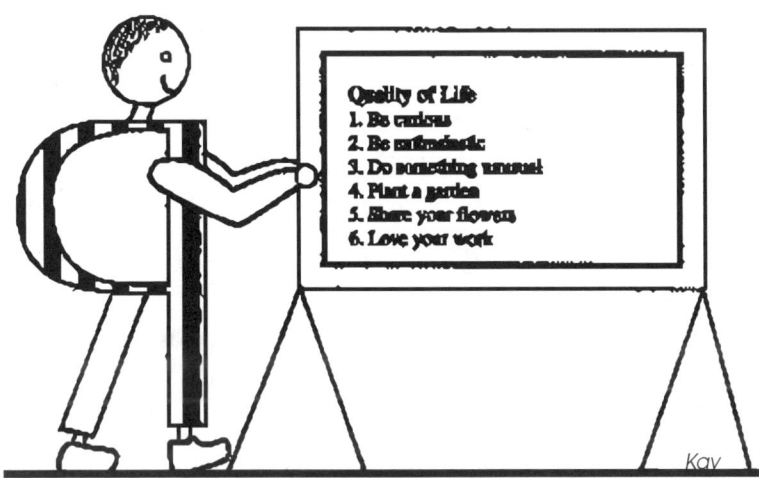

Quality of Life
1. Be curious
2. Be enthusiastic
3. Do something unusual
4. Plant a garden
5. Share your flowers
6. Love your work

Kay

17. Not Enough Hours In A Day

Everyone should be as excited about taking a new job as Howard Coleman was. Howard had been semi-retired for many years when he received a letter from a computer company offering him a job as a Technical Advisor. He wasn't looking for a job and ignored the first letter, but when a second letter arrived he decided to see what the company had to offer. What they had to offer appealed to Howard and he accepted the job; it made no difference to him or to the company that he was 83 years old.

Howard was happy working at his new job for two years until a heart problem sent him to the hospital for surgery. He was anxious to get his heart repaired so that he could get back to his interesting work and all of the other projects he had planned for the future. However, his damaged 85-year-old heart gave out during surgery, bringing to an end a long life of extraordinary achievements.

Howard was born in the Ozarks, but his busy life took him to far-away places. He received his Masters in Electrical Engineering at Oregon State University. He spent much of his adult life with the Army, serving in North Africa with the Allied Forces Headquarters and in Italy, South France, Germany, and Austria.

After the war, Howard and his family lived in Virginia where he was assigned to the Pentagon in Research and Development. His next tour of duty was in Korea as Commander of the 60th Ordinance Group; there he received the Legion of Merit and was promoted to Colonel. Later he was stationed at White Sands Missile Range, Las Cruces, New Mexico, until he retired in 1958.

Soon after retiring from the Army, Howard began another career when he became an assistant professor in the Electrical Engineering Department at New Mexico State University. He taught there until he retired again in 1973.

Howard found pleasure in everything he did, but one of his most enjoyable experiences was spending several weeks traveling with the Hoxie Bros. Circus in the summer of 1970. A friend says about that experience, "Howard was convinced thereafter that he had sawdust in his blood."

Trains, full size or model, in service or in museums, excited Howard. He had an extensive model railroad collection and visited railroad museums wherever he and his wife Edith traveled. At the time of his death he had plans for expanding his model train layout.

Howard and Edith had a mutual interest in raising exotic plants in their garden and greenhouse. They spent many happy hours working side by side planning, planting, and sharing their flowers with friends and neighbors.

Because of his outgoing personality, Howard loved to participate. As a member of Toastmasters he won most of the speech contests he entered. His wide interests and his knowledge of a variety of subjects enabled him to meet every speaking challenge.

Reading was another of Howard's pleasures. According to Edith, "He didn't read just to be reading, but he read extensively about whatever he was working on at the time." He subscribed to railroad magazines and computer magazines as well as others, and he read each issue from cover to cover.

Besides having sawdust in his blood, Howard must have had some chalk there too—"he really liked teaching." He taught CPR for the Red Cross the last five years of his life; he was fascinated by calculators and taught in that field; computers intrigued him and he became a computer whiz.

There weren't enough hours in the day for Howard. He began each day at 6:00 A.M. and didn't stop until 11:00 P.M. or midnight. His last job was ideal for him because he could start making telephone calls to the East Coast at 6:00 A.M. He would have started earlier if the company had allowed it.

Howard was happy at his job with the computer company. "He often spoke," Edith says, "of how nice it was to be in that atmosphere. The morale was high and he had the opportunity to become acquainted with younger engineers. He was able to totally enjoy it and not have the responsibility of meeting quotas."

While Howard was teaching electrical engineering, CPR, calculators and much more, he was also teaching all who knew him how to get the most out of life. He was enthusiastic about everything he did. Until the day he died, Howard was planning projects for the future. He will always be remembered by those who knew him as a wonderful role model for positive aging.

Q = Quality

Inner peace
Good friends
Comfort
Beauty
Wholesome food
Quiet
Leisure
Daydreams
Memories
Blessings to count
Caring people
Helping hands
Pleasant smells
Appreciation
Music
Clean clothes
Hot water
Green grass
Trees
Warmth

Any or all of these can add quality to our lives.

Quality is that special ingredient that makes anything better, including life. The dictionary defines quality as "a degree of excellence." Possessing great wealth is not essential; owning a luxury home is not essential. Howard Coleman's "degree of excellence" meant loving his work, his family, and his special interests— teaching, learning, trains, and circuses.

Being aware of our inner resources can add greatly to the quality of our lives. That awareness is born in quiet times of meditation when we shut out the world and listen to our inner self.

Quality does not mean perfect. Our lives can have a degree of excellence in spite of challenges and mistakes. We can see our mistakes as stepping stones or foundation stones and build on them while we accept ourselves as the unique individuals we are.

Old age can be a time for increased awareness and personal growth. It is a time to reflect and to remember, a time free from the responsibilities of our younger years. We have time to ask the question, "Who am I?" and time to listen for the answer.

As we reflect on what gives our life quality, we may want to add to our list:

Husband or wife
Grandchildren
Pictures of bygone days
Old love letters tied in blue
A scrapbook from grade school
An old report card
A diploma
A Boy Scout badge

Like Howard Coleman, we can be enthusiastic in our work and in our leisure. We can plan for tomorrow, as he did, even though we do not know how many tomorrows we may have. *Now* is the time to experience the greatest possible "degree of excellence" in our lives.

R = Remember

Kay

18. *Looking Back*

Picture a slip of a woman, 91 years old, mowing her large lawn with a push-type mower. Now watch that same small woman sawing her winter's wood supply with her own chain saw. That woman is Maria Schmidt.

Maria lives alone in her pleasant home on the 30-acre wooded lot which she and her husband bought in 1949. Her husband is no longer living; today her two daughters and their families share her lot in homes of their own.

Maria's weeks are full; to get an interview with her requires planning ahead. On Sunday she attends the church where she has been a member for many years. At least one day a week she attends a meeting or study group at the church, and one day is set aside for a shopping trip with a daughter or granddaughter. You don't just "drop in" on Maria because you probably won't find her at home.

Maria treasures rich and happy memories of her childhood and she has an extraordinary ability to recall and relive those days of long ago. Following are some of those memories just as Maria recalled and recorded them:

Summer vacation. Going barefoot all summer long. The dust feeling so good to our feet.

Winter. Walking to school over hedges covered with snowdrifts and sitting around the big stove in the center of the school room.

Watching the clock for 4 o'clock, time to go home.

My 6-year birthday party and beautiful red dress that my Mother made, and because I was important that day, my playmates all wanted to walk beside me.

My Aunt and I in horse and buggy going around the neighborhood to invite the school children.

My swing in our old cottonwood where I swung hour after hour.

Our family around the supper table lighted by a reflector lamp on the wall, the harmony and camaraderie of all.

Thanksgiving where we all got up early hoping for the
first snow.

Christmas—all our stockings (mine, long black ones)
hung on the wainscoting, all eight of them, and
finding them on Christmas morning with candy,
nuts, and a toy or two and on the top an orange
(not a common fruit in those days in the Mid-
dlewest).

Our big red barn where we swung from one side to
the other on a stout rope, from rafter to rafter.

New mown hay with its never forgotten, wonderful
fragrance.

Visiting my grandmother and grandfather in the summer, but so glad to hear the clop, clop of the
horse when my parents came to bring me
home.

That wonderful secure feeling I had when I reached
home, as if a cape was thrown over my shoul-
ders removing all care and worry, physical and
spiritual.

Summer showers. The thunder heads piled high in
the sky. The pelting of the rain on the corn
as it came closer and closer and the sky
darkened.

The chorus of the frogs in the Froelick slough in the
evening.

The street lights in Bloomington seeming like a big city.
Night scenes seldom seen by a country child.

The fireflies in summer flying up and down. Magical
and wondrous.

A week at a camp on the Illinois River when I was about
18 years of age. Rides on the river, dancing at
night, boyfriends a plenty.

In summer, the song of the brown thrush in the hedges,
so shy it was seldom seen.
Picking wild strawberries, tasting their sweetness and
carrying some home to our Mother in our hot
little hands.
Swinging with my brother Jimmy, hearing him singing
his made-up songs.
Picking violets that grew along the little brook behind
the school house, Alice and I, for our teacher.
Coming home late at night, the soft summer darkness
around us, the horse knowing the way on the
darkest night.
On still nights, the magic of the star-filled skies and
the new mown hay with all its fragrance.
Fields of red clover giving sweetness to the air.
Lilacs blooming in the Spring in our backyard.

Our Old House
Where We Were Born

The old house stands way back from the road,
It's brown and ugly and old.
That is to others, but not to me
For I know the story it told.

For it has a past, that old house
Once it was young and fair.
It was filled with laughter and voices then
For a happy family lived there.

The windows shone with a beckoning light
And the doors were opened wide.
There was lots of company in those olden days
And lots of room inside.

For a family of ten needs lots of room
    And lots of space outside
To laugh and play and run all day
    With hardly a care or a sigh.

Oh, it was sweet in the long ago
    To roam so wild and free
Where the soft winds blew o'er the prairie fields
    And the brown thrush sang 'neath the osage tree.

And in the summer the tall corn grew,
    Reaching its green arms to the sky.
The willows grew down the old north lane
    And I walked in their shade as I passed them by.

An old fashioned lilac grew in the back
    Wafting its fragrance on the morning breeze
And the old cottonwood, like a sentinel stood,
    While the south wind whispered and rustled
    its leaves.

There was a row of tall maple trees
    Casting their cool deep shadows below.
Tom Thumb lived in that first old maple,
    Someone told me that I used to know.

The south lane wandered through the pasture green
    To a white gate waiting there.
We sat on the bars and dreamed our dreams
    Longing to go, we knew not where.

At the crossroads stood the one-room school
    Where our teacher taught us the Golden Rule
And the copy-book Maxims so tried and true
    About honor and truth; we learned those, too.

Oh, it would be good to go back for awhile
   Back to those days so rare
To play with my brothers and sisters and find
   My Mother and Father awaiting me there;

But it's only a dream now; it was long, long ago
   And the house looks forsaken and old;
That is, to others, but not to me
   For I have its memories to hold.

Maria Schmidt

R = Remember

"I remember when—." Those three words can unlock a rich storehouse of memories filed in our minds. Even though everything we have ever learned or experienced is filed away as a memory, we can never overload or even fill our minds; their capacity is unlimited.

A myth of aging is that old people are not able to learn or to remember. Many buy into that misinformation and re-enforce it by declaring, "I don't remember as well as I used to." Often people begin saying those words when they are no more than thirty.

Anyone who has lived to 70, 80, 90, or older, has a lifetime of experience stored in his memory bank. My friend who has been in show business for many years talks of memories as "reruns." When he and his show-business friends get together, they "rerun" their earlier years. We do not need a VCR to rerun our memories; they are complete with color, sound and feeling.

In memory, we can retrace the roads we have traveled in life; there have been detours, muddy ruts, quiet country back roads, congested city streets, and smooth, high-speed highways. In retraveling those memory roads, we can relive our childhoods, the people we met, our experiences, our joys and our sorrows.

As we rerun our memories we can edit them—we can fast-forward those which are painful and slow down those we want to savour. We can even put them on "pause" while we are warmed by the joy, love, excitement, and beauty of special experiences. We each have our own memories, different from those of our fellow man; they are what make us unique.

I had the privilege of interviewing and writing the life story of Carl who was 100 when I met him. Carl's keen mind and total recall were fascinating; he grew up in a world far different from today's world. He remembered the exact wage he was paid for his first job, and conversations of seventy and eighty years ago. There never was and never will be another human being with Carl's memories—or yours—or mine.

We are never too old to add to our memory files. Nina Rust (Chapter 4) was still storing memories when, at 109, she rode with her grandson in a Classic Car Parade.

Maria Schmidt makes her memories live through her vivid descriptions of sights, sounds, and feelings. It is plain to see that she enjoys replaying her memories in full color. As Maria has shown us, one of the bonuses of growing old is having the time to rerun our life's experiences on the screens of our minds—having the time to look back and to remember.

19. Seeing With Unseeing Eyes

"Isn't that a beautiful picture? My artist friend painted it for me." Judy Deppman was showing her visitor around her tastefully furnished and decorated apartment, pointing out special objects which she had chosen for their beauty. She spoke as if she could see them, but Judy is blind; she has been totally blind since she was eighteen. Beauty is precious to Judy; she doesn't take it for granted as many sighted people do.

Judy lives by herself in an apartment in Los Angeles, a few blocks from the Braille Institute whose services she credits with saving her life more than twenty years ago when it didn't seem worth saving.

Twenty years ago Judy's marriage was not meeting her needs. She did not know how she could leave her marriage and be able to support herself, her teenage daughter and her guide dog. She was desperate; she sat in her darkness with no one to turn to; nothing to do but listen to the radio. As she contemplated how to get out of her dark world in the least painful way, she heard an announcement which caught her attention—it was a number to call if you were blind and needed help, the number for the Braille Institute. Judy fit both categories—she was blind and she desperately needed help; she knew she had to call that number. She was able to remember the number until she could find a dime and a telephone. The woman who answered her call offered to send someone immediately to talk to Judy. That phone call, according to Judy, marked the beginning of her life.

Today Judy is happy and active. She dresses fashionably, carefully choosing each day's outfit by using a special labeling system she learned for matching her clothes and accessories. Her hair is attractive and her makeup is meticulous.

To compensate for not being able to see, Judy has developed a sensory awareness system which alerts her to the presence of others; she has developed a keen ability to hear, and she has learned to read and write in Braille, a skill that has honed her sense of touch.

Judy is a joy and an inspiration to know. She owns a large library, including a dictionary and Bible embossed in Braille. Philosophy and spirituality are her favorite subjects; she attends lectures on those subjects as well as a variety of other subjects. She attends classes at Los Angeles City College near where she lives. Judy, on staff at the Braille Institute, is a substitute teacher for training adults who are adjusting to blindness.

Judy is not a prisoner in her home. She takes her white cane—after she has dressed carefully and attractively—and off she goes to shop, visit friends, or teach at the Institute. She crosses busy streets by herself, boards a bus, and gets off exactly where she wants to be. "Unless," she says, "the bus driver fails to call the stop. I've learned much about myself in those times when I have been lost." She seems to know instinctively (a result of many years of practice) how far it is from the bus stop to the door of the beauty shop or the store she wants to visit. She walks with an air of confidence with her head up.

An annual trip to Virginia to visit her daughter, son and grandchildren is one of Judy's special pleasures. She also flies to other cities to visit friends and has been "sightseeing" in Hawaii. She and her daughter recently flew to Jamaica where they boarded a cruise ship for a relaxing eight days in the Caribbean.

Judy's visitor is surprised when she says, "I saw a good movie yesterday; you should see it." Or when she talks about a television program which she has "seen." In her latest hard-to-believe adventure, Judy has commissioned her artist friend to copy a picture which she had admired in her daughter's home. She describes the picture in detail and is excited about hanging it in her home with her other pictures.

One evening two sighted friends accompanied Judy and her gentleman friend—her blind friend—to a posh hotel for dinner and dancing. After the sighted couple had toured the dance floor with them, pointing out where potted plants and nearby tables were located, they were on their own and had a wonderful time swaying and rocking to the rhythm of the music. Their dexterity in handling their food and silverware, as well as wine glasses, water glasses, and coffee cups, was amazing.

Judy types letters to her friends, including typing the addresses on the envelopes. She has that information, and much more, embossed in Braille on her well-organized file cards. Nothing stops Judy—she has recently learned to use a computer which she finds exciting and a great help with her writing.

"One of the purposes for my being on earth," Judy concludes, "is to inspire people. I seem to be able to instill that little extra push or whatever it is to make them want to go on. So maybe that's my gift—to inspire, no more, no less. Life is really good to me. I find that if you are good to Life, Life is good to you."

Although Judy is blind, she sees more through her senses, her imagination and her heart than most of us see with 20-20 vision.

S = See

My thesaurus lists many words as synonyms for "see." Too often we limit ourselves to a narrow definition of a word. If our definition for "see" means only physically seeing and we do not have that ability, we believe we are handicapped. Judy, however, is not handicapped because she has defined "see" in other ways, beyond what her eyes can see.

We all agree that sight is a precious gift; nevertheless, Judy and others are proof that it is possible to live fully, happily, and independently in spite of blindness. They have found ways to compensate by using their other senses. Judy sees through her imagination and through the eyes of others. Her hands become her eyes as she reads the raised symbols of Braille. She listens more closely than a sighted person and has trained her ears to become substitutes for her eyes.

Failing eyesight is often a natural consequence of aging. Those of us who had 20/20 vision when we were younger may find our sight diminishing as our years are increasing. The invention of Braille embossing by Louis Braille, in 1829, was a big step toward opening doors for the blind. Today, sophisticated computers perform miracles far beyond Louis Braille's wildest dreams.

Judy and others who live fully in spite of disabilities are positive examples for all of us. Each person's story is one of courage; each has achieved his independence through struggle, hard work, and patience. Through them we have learned that even if our eyes do not "see", nothing can rob us of the ability to imagine, picture, and visualize with our mind's eye. We can live fully!

T = Travel

Kay

20. Have Suitcase Will Travel

"Have suitcase, will travel" is Cleona Ternes' motto. Cleona is a late-blooming traveler—she didn't pack her suitcase until she was past seventy; until then she was house-bound, child-bound, job-bound, and civic organization-bound. She doesn't complain; those were her responsibilities and she accepted them.

Cleona is a native Californian. She and her husband owned and operated an office supply company in Northern California all their married life. Their son, an only child, became active in the business when he was sixteen and assumed full ownership after his father died in 1977. Cleona continues to work in the business four days a week, reserving the right to take time off to travel.

Cleona's roots grow deep in the city where she lives; she moved there with her parents when she was barely two. Her present home is one which she and her husband had built when they were married in 1937; next door is a house built by her father in which her parents lived for sixty years.

In her "bound" years, Cleona found an outlet for her artistic talents by taking oil-painting classes at night. A colorful seascape, painted by Cleona, hangs in her living room. She taught herself to carve wood, soapstone, and featherstone, and found that carving fit into her busy lifestyle more easily than painting because she could stop at any stage without having to clean her brushes and put her paints away.

Cleona took photography classes and joined a camera club where she "won a couple of awards." "But," she admits, "picture taking doesn't satisfy me like carving does."

"Volunteering" was Cleona's middle name before she put on her traveling shoes. She served on the Recreation Commission for several years and worked in the Well-Baby Clinic; she collected for the March of Dimes and other worthy causes; and she acted as secretary in every club she joined—PTA, BPW and Women's Clubs.

The day finally arrived when Cleona was free to travel. But who would be her travel companion? She found the answer to that question when she decided,

"If you don't have anybody to go with, go by yourself." She took a trial trip—three days in Yosemite—to see how she would like being alone and she "found it would work out very nicely." It was an opportunity to know herself better and to make new friends.

Since Cleona had waited seventy years to travel, the next question was where to begin. She chose for her first trip, following the brief one to Yosemite, to travel the inside waterways from Savannah, Georgia, to Baltimore, Maryland. It was a beautiful and an enjoyable time spent on rivers, lakes and bays and Cleona was bitten by the travel-bug.

As her next travel experience, shared with her sister and brother-in-law, Cleona flew to England where she and her companions rented a car to tour England, Scotland and Wales. Soon she visited Canada, Tahiti, Australia, New Zealand, and Hawaii. She has seen the United States from the canyons, rivers and parks in the West to the fall foliage in New England. A special Thanksgiving marked her first visit to Florida.

Cleona answered quickly when asked what has been her favorite trip so far, "My trip to Africa. I loved it. I don't think anything I would ever do could top that."

On her most recent tour, Cleona and a friend flew to England, West Germany, Poland, Russia, Holland, Finland, Norway and Denmark. Of all the places they visited, Poland made the greatest impression on her. She found that the people of Poland are proud of their independence and their country.

Although Cleona has traveled by luxury liner, she "prefers the smaller boats." She explained her choice, "When I travel, I go to see new things and meet new people. I don't care particularly for party time." Cleona had a hip replacement in 1981 which prevents her from scaling mountains; she doesn't mind, she just sits at the base and admires the view.

Less conventional means of travel also appeal to Cleona. She has looked down on the earth from a hot-air balloon and has had the courage to ride a glider; now she is eagerly anticipating her first ride in a helicopter.

In spite of working and traveling, Cleona finds time to enjoy her garden. Most of her rose bushes are as firmly rooted as she is, as they were moved to their present location in 1949 when the house was moved there. Cleona's yard has flowers blooming year-round, but springtime is the best, when her garden is a riot of color and beauty.

Cleona's many interests keep her busy, and she declares firmly, "I will never have to worry about being bored. I get very annoyed when I hear someone say they are bored." If she isn't off on another sightseeing tour, she will be enjoying her grandchildren and great-grandchildren or she will be working in her rose garden. She is determined that those deep-rooted rose bushes will be there for the next generation to enjoy.

T = Travel

Travel—the very word has a golden aura around it. When we hear the word "travel" our minds and imaginations immediately begin to pack our suitcases. We think of exotic places with exotic names—Tahiti, Casablanca, Rio.

Ask almost any of us on retirement day what we plan to do with our new leisure and we will answer with the exciting word—"travel." We now have time to board our magic carpet and take off to explore new places, have new adventures, and meet interesting people.

But we have choices to make before we bid our homes and friends "good-bye":

Where do we want to go?

How do we plan to get there?

Who would be a good travel companion?

Before we fly off in just any direction, let's consider those questions.

Where do we want to go? Even if we have traveled extensively there must be someplace left to visit. Think of the most far-out place you can imagine—Antarctica, Timbuktu—have you been there?

How do we plan to get there? Maybe we are not physically able to handle the rigors of traveling—getting to airports, driving on freeways, and handling our luggage. Maybe our finances will not allow us to pay for a cruise on a luxury liner or to buy a ticket on a plane flying to a foreign land.

Who would be a good travel companion? We may, like Cleona, find that we enjoy traveling alone. The time alone could be an excellent opportunity to enjoy our own company and to become better acquainted with ourselves.

If we do not have answers to those questions, does that mean we have to give up our dreams of traveling? How can we go places and do things without flying, sailing, or driving; without spending great amounts of money; and without a travel companion?

Does traveling always mean physically going to another place? No, there are other ways to travel. We can sit in our own homes and travel via our imaginations; we can visit any country on the face of the earth through books, maps, pictures, and by talking to those who have lived there. We can learn about the people, their culture, their geography, and their language without ever leaving the comfort of our easy chairs.

If we have been bemoaning the fact that we lack money for traveling or have physical challenges, it is time to consider alternatives. By using our imaginations and creativity, we can travel widely and those excursions may prove to be some of our most enjoyable and adventurous. Let's pack our bags, real or imaginary; there will never be a better time to begin exploring places we have only dreamed of until today.

U = Use Your Talents

Kay

21. Releasing The Beauty Within

Ben—his given name is Burnett Gibson Dirks—sees beauty in a piece of wood that someone else would use as fuel in the fireplace. Ben creates sculptures from driftwood which he finds on the beach or picks up in the forest. Redwood is his favorite material. Ben believes it is important to leave the wood in its natural shape; he does not cut or carve it; he polishes it after he has removed the bark and other extraneous materials.

Ben's forefathers were pioneers; his paternal great-grandfather was a shipbuilder who came to San Francisco from Holland; his grandfather and father were also shipbuilders. Ben's maternal grandmother came across the plains in a covered wagon caravan organized by her father who died before he reached California, never realizing his dream of beginning a new life in a new land. His 14-year-old son assumed his father's role and brought the family to California.

Ben tells interesting stories about his early days in Butchertown, then a district in San Francisco. His parents had a dairy before they moved into town. His mother didn't want to leave the cow behind, so Ben, his dad, and his brother walked, leading the cow, from their dairy to their new home, a distance of approximately thirty miles. A cow would have a busy time dodging cars today as that area is solid freeways and parking lots.

Ben admits that he was a bit of a problem child; his parents chose to send him to military school where he would receive strict discipline. He earned his room and board by cleaning toilets and classrooms, and he got up early every morning to start a fire in the furnace. Ben learned his lesson; he graduated from high school with a football scholarship to the University of Washington.

A degree in physical education opened the door for Ben to work for a year or two for the City of Seattle Parks Commission. He had planned to be a coach, but there were few coaching jobs in those Depression years. His father had abandoned the family leaving Ben as the breadwinner which meant he had to take a job in a flour mill to support his mother and younger brother.

His job in the mill did not give Ben the opportunity to use his in-born talents—he was born to be a builder just as his forefathers had been. He recalls that as a child he was "the most popular kid on the block" when he made wagons, kites, stilts, and scooters on roller skates for the other kids.

After working a few years in the flour mill, Ben chose to leave the mill and become a carpenter. He enjoyed working with wood and soon earned enough money to buy a house for his mother and help his brother attend college. Ben is proud that he played a part in helping his brother get a college degree and become an educator.

Ben's big heart led him to support his sister and her children until he was married and had a family of his own. He and his wife had three children; they were a happy family until she died of cancer when their youngest child was fifteen.

All of Ben's talents and creativity were put to good use when he built an adobe house for his family. He was inspired to build of adobe when he studied early California history in high school and was intrigued by the adobe missions.

Ben designed the three-bedroom, two-bath house and literally built it from the ground up. For three years he searched the area where he lived to find the type of dirt which would make the best bricks. He bought an old truck to haul the dirt to the building site and he rebuilt an old bread mixer to mix the dirt and water. He made two bricks at a time by filling a frame with mud; when the bricks were set he removed them and let them dry in the sun. In addition to making the bricks, he made the shakes for the roof, did all of the carpentry work, and laid the floor of six-inch Spanish tile. Using this slow process took Ben five years to build his house. It was indeed "the house that Ben built."

Ben retired at sixty-two and used his extra time to build another house. He used lumber instead of adobe and built this house in six months, doing most of the work himself.

His driftwood sculpture hobby began while Ben was working in Seattle in the flour mill; his sister-in-law was his teacher. He enjoyed his hobby until he had to put it away to work full time as a carpenter. Recently Ben found the time and the need for his former hobby. "I began working with driftwood again," he says, "because I quit drinking and smoking and I had to have something to keep me busy."

Ben doesn't sell his pieces—he gives them away. He needs to begin selling them or giving more of them away as he is being pushed out of his home by driftwood. He buys used tables and stools which he rebuilds into revolving bases to display his sculptures.

Environmental regulations, especially in California, limit the amount of driftwood allowed to be taken from parks and beaches. Because Oregon's restrictions are not quite so rigid, Ben occasionally travels north to replenish his supply.

"I am what they call a 'boner'." Ben explains. "After the wood is ready to be polished, I take a deer horn and rub it until it comes out shining as if I had varnished it. That makes it unique. I am no carver; I leave the wood as natural as it is and take it from there. I don't disfigure the wood. If Nature wanted it to be that way, that's what I want it to be. I don't try to make my sculptures look like something, but some of them do if you use your imagination. Some people see a bird or an animal which I can't see."

Ben shares his knowledge and skills as a volunteer at a senior center where he teaches other seniors how to release the beauty in driftwood.

Like many other retired people, Ben says, "I used to play golf, ski and do other things, but I don't have time now. I still fish, though." He confesses that he would like to build another house someday. He still has talents begging to be used. Did I mention that Ben is a young 83?

U = Use Your Talents

"I can't do anything special—I'm justa housewife."
—"I'm justa secretary."
—"I'm justa old man (or woman)."

No person is a "justa." Every person has special talents. We do not always recognize and acknowledge our talents; nevertheless, we have them and we can use them if we stop labeling ourselves a "justa."

Too often, talent is believed to be only the ability to paint, write, sculpt, sing, dance, or act. Talent is much more—it is "any natural or special gift or aptitude." *Natural* is the important word in that definition. Just because we *are*, we have natural abilities and aptitudes; it is up to us to recognize them and to use them.

Any one of us who has lived sixty years or more cannot be a "justa." We have years of experiences, adventures, memories and accumulated wisdom.

Using talents is not limited to physical abilities. We may not be physically able to get out of bed, but we can still use our talents. My friend, Doris, lives in a nursing home; she is bedridden and never leaves her room. In spite of her physical limitations, however, Doris has found a way to use her talents. The woman who shares her room is often confused and unable to make her needs understood to the hospital staff. Doris understands her and acts as her interpreter. Doris also contributes to the friendly atmosphere of the home by using her talents for cheerfulness and cooperation. These are truly talents.

Listening—really listening—is a talent. Listening does not require eyes that see or legs that walk—it requires only ears that hear, a heart that understands, and a mind that is open and non-judgmental.

Reading aloud is a talent, one which can be used, for instance, to broaden a child's world of understanding. Good readers are needed to record books for those who cannot see or have never learned to read.

Visiting is a talent. As the song says, "People need people." Many people in hospitals, nursing homes, and retirement homes have outlived their families and friends and have no visitors. That is a perfect place for us to use our visiting talents. We don't even have to discuss the latest political or economic crisis; just being there and listening is what is important.

Living positively is a talent. The people whose stories I have told in this book are living their talents in many different ways. One can make driftwood sculpture; one can paint on ceramic tiles; one can play the piano; one can be friendly—one talent is no more special than the other.

If we have been telling ourselves that we have no talents, it is time to think again. No matter what age we are, now is the time to know, "I am a person with talents." Now is the time to use those talents in ways that will add meaning to our lives and to the lives of others.

V = Volunteer

Kay

22. *Friendship Makes A Happy Heart*

The nameplate on her desk at Creekside Convalescent Hospital reads, "Gladys Barnes, Patient Coordinator." Those words are short for "A volunteer who can be called on day or night." Gladys spends many nights at the hospital sitting beside a dying patient. "I hold their hands and pray with them," Gladys says, "because they need somebody to be with them. They seem to be more peaceful if they know someone is sitting with them."

When I asked Gladys how long she has been volunteering her talents, services, and love, she answered, "It has been so long, I don't even remember." She does remember that she worked in a convalescent hospital when she was thirteen, but admits, "I was getting paid for that, so that doesn't count." What does count is that Gladys, no longer thirteen but seventy, still works in a convalescent hospital—she volunteers her services.

Gladys is affectionately known as "Mother Witch." That name is a result of the many Halloween parties Gladys and her late husband, Ben, gave for thirty-five years in an effort to create a "Safe Halloween" for children in their city. Early parties were held on their front porch, but they became so popular that they filled the whole big yard. Gladys and Ben went all out—they decorated the yard with fluorescent and black lights; they had witches and goblins, jack-o-lanterns of every size and shape, and plenty of goodies for the children and grown-ups.

For many of those years, Gladys and Ben financed the parties themselves by holding rummage sales in the downtown area and at their home. When their parties became famous and too large and expensive for them to handle by themselves, downtown stores donated items "and people would be bringing things by all year long." They began planning the next year's party the day after Halloween.

When Ben died seven years ago, Gladys was left to carry on the Halloween tradition by herself. She shares Halloween at schools and other hospitals, and plans an elaborate party at Creekside Convalescent Hospital. Reporters and T.V. crews are there to cover the festivities.

Because she spends so much of her time there, Gladys has her own desk at the hospital. The story of her life is posted on the bulletin board behind her desk—a photograph of Ben hangs beside their wedding picture; there are numerous Certificates of Recognition and Congratulations attesting to Gladys' contribution to community projects. One card sums up Gladys' philosophy in its message, "Friendship Makes a Happy Heart." One of Gladys' proudest possessions, a letter from President Reagan, accompanied an award for her outstanding volunteering.

Gladys has no time for idleness—she is hostess and past president of the local Chapter and Council of International Training Communication (ITC); she belongs to NAACP and is a Commander of Disabled American Veterans Auxiliary (DAVA). She is on the Board of Directors of the Senior Center where she participates in the Silver Spoons Chorus and the Footlight Drama Club. She works regularly at the Senior Center Thrift Shop, is a member of the Unity Church, and volunteers for RESPITE, an organization devoted to making life better for people with Alzheimers and for their caregivers. Another pet project is LITA—Love Is The Answer—an organization whose purpose is to improve the quality of life of the elderly through one-to-one friendships.

Gladys' association with Creekside Convalescent Hospital began seven years ago when Ben became a patient and eventually died there. Gladys remembers that the day Ben died her minister took her to breakfast and to the mortuary, then he started to take her to her home. "I didn't want to go home," she admits, "so I had him bring me back here to Creekside and I have been here ever since. They needed me and I needed them. I don't have any family; they are my family."

V = Volunteer

Someone needs you; someone needs me, and we both need to be needed. Volunteering is a way to meet those needs. Volunteering our time, our services, and ourselves pays dividends which do not depend on how *much* we give, but on our willingness to give.

Volunteer means to choose to serve, and it has its own rewards—the volunteer receives as much or more than he gives. Gladys Barnes chooses to serve at a convalescent hospital; she, in turn, receives appreciation, recognition, and satisfaction.

The concept of volunteering is a fairly new one. Because most men and women of previous generations did not live as long as we live today, they did not know the luxury of retirement and they did not have free time to use as they wished.

We volunteer for various reasons: because we like people, because we receive satisfaction, or because we see a need to be filled. Although volunteers are not seeking credit, organizations appreciate them and recognize them in some special way—with a luncheon, a dinner, or an award.

If all volunteering were to end today, the world would be a sorry place; many organizations could not survive without people willing to give their time and themselves. Older people can be found on the front lines in the army of volunteers: they speak for fundraisers, stuff envelopes, visit in hospitals, push wheelchairs, listen and encourage. Others serve in city, county, and state government where they represent and advocate for seniors. Still others serve on Library Boards and act as docents at museums. Senior Centers depend on their volunteers.

More and more retirees are tutoring and substituting as foster grandmothers and grandfathers, giving children an opportunity to know their elders in a positive way.

We may choose to volunteer as an extension of the profession in which we were involved in our career. Besides giving us the opportunity to use the experience, expertise, knowledge, and talents we accumulated in our working years, it gives us a sense of continuity in our lives. The next time we feel bored, have nothing to do, and our lives seem to lack purpose, we need only to look around to find a place that is waiting for us, and we won't have to look far. We will soon find ourselves fulfilled and will wonder what we did before we became a member of that army of busy, happy people.

W = Write, Work

Kay

23. Faithful Worker, Talented Writer

There isn't a company in the world that couldn't use an employee as faithful as Mark Johnson. I met Mark when I went to work for the DuPont Company twenty years ago. At that time Mark had already chalked up more than twenty years with the Company. When I had worked for sixteen years I retired, but not Mark! Now, however, at the age of 75 and after more than forty years with the Company, Mark has decided to hang up his hat and avoid the daily battle of the freeways.

As well as being a faithful worker, Mark is a talented writer. When we were business associates, Mark shared some of his serious and his humorous writings with me. I believed he had a special gift for using words and encouraged him to have his pieces published, but he assured me that he writes for the satisfaction he gets from expressing himself and for the sheer pleasure of writing.

Mark has had a long-time love affair with writing. He remembers being assigned to write an article when he was in seventh grade. Although he doesn't remember the specific topic or what he wrote, he does remember that he was assigned, "the job of collating, indexing and referencing. In fact, I was listed as 'Editor' of the class collage." The "book" he edited went into the college library and, "It may still be there."

After Mark graduated from high school, even before he had started college, he was asked to be editor of the college paper, "the first time it had ever been done by less than a Junior." As a college student, Mark received an "A" in a Journalism class which he seldom attended because he was hanging out in the print shop where he received "hands-on" training for many aspects of the production of the paper/magazine.

According to Mark, "A big part of the writing gig is the fun of playing with words." For example:

> Siftings from My Accretion of Scribbled Squibs:
>
> Possible ideas—mostly stillborn—pending Evaluation, Expansion or Expiation.
>
> Lamentable Launchings, Languishing for Aborting or Interring.

Unstrung Bangles, Bungles, Baubles and Beads:

One man's total, Teflon truth is another man's silly, senseless superstition.

If you doubt the advantage of the Metric System, multiply MDCLII times CDLXXIV.

For years I pondered: "Is having an open mind the same as being empty headed? Now I wonder: Does being 'bilingual' mean the same as 'speaking with forked tongue'?"

Mark enjoys humor. He collects cartoons and funny quips which he posts on the bulletin board above his desk. You might guess that Mark's favorite page in the Reader's Digest is "Laughter, the Best Medicine."

Although Mark was once a professional photographer, he now takes pictures only for his own enjoyment and to share with his friends. His camera takes pictures in three dimensions; when the transparencies are viewed through a special stereoscopic viewer, the figures look as though they could be touched. His large collection includes pictures taken while traveling in many countries and those taken when he was official photographer of a World War II expedition exploring the Greenland Icecap.

Talk about a lucky break for a photographer!—Mark held the winning ticket in a drawing for a trip to Europe several years ago. He took many pictures on that trip. He and his wife have cruised to Alaska and the Orient; they have traveled by auto, bus and train to Canada and Mexico, and have visited most of the fifty states.

In spite of some health problems that would set most of us back on our heels, Mark has continued to work long past the generally accepted retirement age. With the new leisure he will enjoy after he retires, Mark may get around to having his writings published. I hope he does.

W = Write, Work

Many of us list the word "work" with the other not-so-nice four-letter words. It does not belong in that category—it belongs in the list of good things about life. Through our work we have the opportunity to interact with our fellowman, to use our brains and our muscles, and to contribute to our world. Work is a force for good, not for evil.

Leo Buscaglia, in his book *Bus 9 to Paradise*, reminds us, ". . . few of us realize how much happiness is dependent upon our work. We complain that we have too much work, that it's just so much drudgery, but we fail to realize it's our work that keeps us alert and growing, and helps us to maintain our dignity . . . Work of any kind offers many rewards . . . It keeps us in human company. It brings us into life. It requires us to experience new things."[1]

An older person, with his years of experience and training, often makes a better worker than a younger one. The older worker has accumulated know-how; he has learned to be responsible for being on the job everyday; and he has learned the importance of coop-

---

[1] Buscaglia, Leo. *Bus 9 to Paradise*. William Morrow and Co., Inc., New York, NY, 1986.

eration. Just as "no man is an island," no man (or woman) works alone.

Unlike the generations before us, we live at a time when many of us are privileged to retire with a pension. We have been able to save a portion of our earnings to use when we are no longer in the daily "off-to-work" routine. Do not think, however, that retirement is the end of working—retirement is just a new kind of job. To make it a busy, full, and rewarding time, we must work at it by planning, finding new interests and new ways to be creative. We have the advantage of more time to realize our dreams.

Writing may be one way to realize a dream. Writing, like working, gives us a purpose and a challenge. It is a way to create which requires diligence and discipline while it returns dividends.

A keen and lively interest in life—not a college degree—is the only prerequisite for being a writer. Every author does not become wealthy from his work, but most experience pleasure and satisfaction. The activity of writing keeps our brains healthy and our creative juices flowing. Like Mark Johnson, we do not have to be published; we enjoy most that which we write for ourselves.

There are no age limits to writing. No law decrees that the retirement age for writers is 65 or any other age.

Many excellent books have been written on the subject of writing. Among my favorites are:

Peter Elbow's *Writing with Power*

Natalie Goldberg's *Writing Down the Bones*

Brenda Ueland's *If You Want To Write*

If you think you cannot write, you are mistaken—
you can! And you cannot begin any younger. When you
take up pen and paper, you will be amazed at the
words that you find buried deep within, just waiting
to be set free. Try it! Today may be the day you dis-
cover a talent you did not dream you had.

X = 'Xpect

Kay

24. Keep Your Sense Of Humor

From Boondocks, California, to Broadway, New York. That, in a nut shell, is the story of Jack Williams' life. Jack can hardly believe that he went from growing up in a logging camp in Northern California to dancing in major shows on Broadway.

Jack admires the courage of his ancestors who left their homes in the East to become part of the gold-rush in the West. His mother's parents came over the

Santa Fe Trail while his father's parents traveled the Oregon Trail.

A one-room school in a logging camp was Jack's introduction to education. He graduated from one room to a multi-room school when his parents left the logging camp to move into a city. A ballroom dancing class in the junior high school gymnasium started him on his way to Broadway when he did not even know there was such a place. A teacher recognized his exceptional talent and suggested to his parents that they provide him with dancing lessons. Jack loved to dance and chose to study tap even though he "got ribbed by the kids in school."

"Each year," Jack remembers, "the tiny dancing school would have a dance review and that was the biggest thing that could happen. For three days the theater was packed because there was no other entertainment. We were stars."

Jack learned quickly; his mother soon decided that he was ready for more advanced training and began taking him to San Francisco every weekend. When he was sixteen he moved into the City to continue his lessons. His first job required him to be a singer, dancer, and men's-room attendant, all for the sumptuous sum of $15 a week for three shows a night, seven nights a week.

The story of Jack's dancing at the most prestigious club in San Francisco, the Peacock Court of the Mark Hopkins Hotel, is much like Hawthorne's legend of The Great Stone Face. As Jack looked at the Peacock Court from the window of his room in the YMCA, he dreamed of dancing there someday—it could only be a dream, an impossible dream. Just as most impossible dreams are realized in unlikely ways, his dream began to become a reality when he moved to Hollywood to dance at a club on the Sunset Strip. There he met the manager of the Mark Hopkins who invited him to return to San Francisco for an engagement. Jack, only seventeen, was sure the manager was teasing him—Jack danced solo and the Mark Hopkins hired team dancers. The manager was persistent. Still only half believing this was a genuine offer, Jack signed a contract for two weeks at the Mark Hopkins and his dream came true.

That two-week engagement at the mark Hopkins was the first step on his way "up." Jack's love of dancing, his talent, and his hard work took him to the most popular clubs in San Francisco, Los Angeles, Chicago, and New York. Then, like many young men at that time, Jack was drafted and Uncle Sam became his manager.

Jack continued to dance, however. He was chosen to be a member of a troupe who traveled and performed in an Air Force show, "Winged Victory," which raised millions of dollars for Air Force relief. Following "Winged Victory," Jack played in "O.K. USA"; he danced with that group at the Potsdam Conference for Joseph Stalin, Clement Atlee, and President Truman.

Upon his discharge from the Air Force Jack returned to Broadway where he appeared on stage with well-known actors and actresses. He met his wife Eleanor on Broadway; she was singing and he was dancing. Jack and Eleanor have been married forty years.

Jack reached a turning point in his life when he injured his knees and was not able to dance for several years. Dancing was Jack's life; without it he became despondent and questioned his reason for living. A friend from his early years visited Jack in New York and was sorry to see him so unhappy. In an effort to help him, his friend invited Jack to return to the city where he grew up to open a liquor store in a new shopping mall. Jack accepted the invitation and gave up dancing completely, devoting the next ten years to his store before he retired.

Soon after he retired, Jack received a phone call from Hollywood inviting him to attend a meeting of the National Endowment of the Arts. At that meeting he was given the opportunity to participate in making a film in which he would dance and talk about his years on Broadway. That film and others were being made to preserve the history of Broadway in the '40s and '50s. They were to be placed on file in the Library of Congress, at Lincoln Center, and in the Film Library in Hollywood.

It had been more than ten years since Jack had danced, but he was confident that he "could get right back in there. But I couldn't." He was devastated but determined. He *would* dance again! After long hours and days of arduous practice Jack "finally got back to dancing" and made the hour-long film.

"That," according to Jack, "got me back to dancing and I haven't stopped." He travels to Hollywood every two months to teach. When his star pupil won an Emmy and gave Jack much of the credit, Jack knew his decision to resume dancing had been the right decision.

Jack's agility and precision make it hard to believe that he is seventy-three. He is not taking a chance on losing his dancing skills again and can be found early in the morning, twice a week, practicing his routines at the local Senior Center.

Jack is an art collector with a special fascination for clowns; he is the proud owner of a clown picture painted by Red Skelton. Jack and Eleanor are regulars at the symphony, ballet, and opera; they have a keen interest in world affairs and believe everyone should be concerned about what is going on in the world.

Jack's philosophy is simple—"Live one day at a time and keep your sense of humor. A sense of humor gets you through dark times." Jack speaks from personal experience. He and Eleanor are a vital, busy, happy couple who expect to enjoy new experiences as they continue to keep in touch with friends from their years on Broadway and as they continue to make new friends. They do not know what tomorrow will bring, but they expect it will be something that will add to their already rich life.

X = 'Xpect

This is an exciting time to live! It is a time of discovery, of fantastic inventions, of medical advancements, of outer and inner exploration, and a time of living longer. This is probably the most exciting period in history; it is our privilege to be a part of it and to expect even more in the years ahead.

In the past, we believed that aging meant traveling a downhill course, with each added year promising fewer adventures and fewer rewards. We believed when we reached fifty, that was it! If we had not made it socially and financially and found happiness, we never would. Not true! Many of us are truly *beginning* to live when we reach fifty and we will continue on that upward course for the rest of our lives. Expecting exciting experiences has no age limits. The combination of exciting experiences and older years may be an idea whose time has come. We are the first generation who can expect to live beyond seventy, eighty, ninety, or even one hundred. A birthday cake blazing with one hundred candles is not unusual today.

There is much to look forward to if we believe there is. If we bless the past, let it go, and know that there is much life still to be lived, that will be true. Regardless of what has happened in the past, today is the first day of the rest of our lives. Each new day brings its own opportunities and experiences.

Today's world is a far different world than that in which our grandparents lived. Imagine, for a minute, our grandparents coming to visit us today—they would be amazed at the things we take for granted. When we imagine seeing our world through their eyes we become aware of the marvels around us; we feel the excitement of living today, and know that we can expect even more tomorrow.

What might I, as an individual, expect in the future? There is surely a person I have not met who will become a good friend, someone with whom I can share stories of our pasts; we can share knowledge we have accumulated over the years; and we can share our philosophies of life. I expect further breakthroughs in medicine, maybe even a cure for cancer in my lifetime. I expect to see new modes of transportation, on the ground as well as in space, and I expect to use new forms of communication.

Some of us may have physical limitations, but that does not stop us from expecting interesting experiences. Mary Hartzog's physical world (Chapter 15) is limited, nevertheless, her mental and social worlds bring her fulfillment through her friendships, television, watching her plants grow and bloom; through reading and learning. She even analyzes her birds in an attempt to determine why the blue parakeet likes the green parakeet better than the other blue one; and why her canary is noisy and scolds so much. She expects and finds pleasure in her limited physical world.

Exciting experiences abound outside and within us, but we can miss them completely if we do not maintain an expectant attitude. Life doesn't hand us interesting experiences on a silver platter, it offers us the opportunity to create them for ourselves.

Y = You

Kay

25. You Are Your Own Best Friend

Discovering who lives under our skin and inside our head is difficult, but it is something we need to do before we can truly know ourselves. Socrates made it sound easy when he admonished, "Know thyself," as if it were a simple thing to do.

Ellen Shay can tell you that knowing one's self is not easy; she has been struggling with Socrates' "simple" admonition all of her 85 years. Ellen grew up in a home which "was filled with hate and anger." Although she didn't know it then, she realizes now that her mother was emotionally ill. Ellen could hardly wait to get away from home; she believed there must be a happier place and a better way to live.

In her childhood Ellen was a loner. She did not want to bring friends to her unhappy home; consequently, she solved that problem by not making friends. As a lonely teenager, she looked forward to going away to college as a means of escape. When she reached college age, however, there was no money for more than the bare necessities for the family. She could attend a tuition-free Normal School and learn to be a teacher, but she did not want to teach; nevertheless, it was a chance to get away from home and she took it. When she had completed two years at Normal School, Ellen obtained a teaching position.

Ellen had taught for three years when she met her husband. He, like Ellen, had grown up in an unhappy home. They were married in 1929, convinced that their troubled childhoods would be a common bond on which they could build a successful marriage. It was a mistake. The old adage, "Two wrongs never make a right" might be paraphrased in their case to say, "Two troubled childhoods never make a happy marriage."

Ellen's husband persuaded her to work while he attended school; he promised she would have her turn after he had graduated and become established. They lived in a furnished room and she worked as a waitress while he earned a Bachelors degree at Columbia, followed by a Masters in Economics at Georgetown University. When he graduated they moved back to New York. In those Depression years, teachers who

148

had jobs hung onto them, making it impossible for Ellen to find a teaching position and forcing her to continue working as a waitress.

In spite of their agreement that Ellen would have her turn to attend college, that time never came. Her ambitious husband bought a building which he and a partner remodeled into furnished rooms with a private tutoring school on one floor. Ellen helped her husband maintain the building and the school.

It was soon apparent that their "common bond of troubled childhoods" was not a solid foundation for marriage and they were divorced. As part of the settlement, Ellen received the building and the school which she tried to manage by herself. Although she worked long, hard hours, mounting costs made it impossible to continue and she had to close the school.

With no family or friends for a support system, this failure was almost more than Ellen could handle. She told herself, however, "There must be a better way to live; life can't be this way all the time." She was determined to find that better way; she wanted to change the picture she saw of her troubled self into a picture of peace and contentment.

Ellen took the first positive step in a new direction when she contacted Dr. Norman Vincent Peale at his church in New York; she had heard that Dr. Peale's church provided free counseling for people seeking to make changes in their lives. Since changing her life was exactly what Ellen wanted to do, she began several years of counseling. She credits that experience with getting her started on the path to understanding herself.

Ellen made another positive step when she taught herself shorthand and typing and took a class in accounting. Those skills enabled her to get more satisfying jobs which more adequately met her financial needs.

After working at a variety of jobs for several years, Ellen decided she wanted to get away from the city. She answered an ad for a secretarial position at a college in a small town in Upstate New York and was hired. Ellen remembers thinking, when she arrived, "I'm home! It was beautiful and the air was clear. Oh boy, it was lovely! It was October and the leaves were changing colors. It was the most beautiful place I have ever seen in my life."

Ellen was "so happy with that job" and would like to have lived and worked there forever. Her job and happiness, however, came to an abrupt halt when she became sixty-five and had to retire as was the mandatory rule in 1970.

Working at the college had given Ellen the opportunity to spend two-week vacations at the University of Kentucky in Lexington. She loved taking classes at the "first college in the United States that would let seniors go to college free." That free college for seniors was the forerunner of Elderhostel.

One of Ellen's summer classes was a writers' workshop. Before the course began, each participant was required to submit an original article for evaluation. Ellen's article, a story about her Dad, was chosen as an example of good writing and was reproduced to be used by the entire class. The well-known author, Jessamyn West, one of the instructors, knew Ellen's story was exceptionally good and encouraged her to have it published. Ellen intended to, but the years went by and she never had it published. She may have forfeited her chance for fame.

After she retired, Ellen traveled with a woman from California whom she had met at the writers' workshop. When they returned to the United States after several months in Spain, Portugal, England, and Majorca, her friend urged her to come to California; she agreed to come for a visit and liked it so much she decided to stay.

Ellen's first home in California was a mobile home outside the congestion of the city. She lived in that home eight years until her eyesight began to fail and she knew she had to move someplace where she could ride the bus; she could no longer see well enough to drive. She sold her mobile home and bought one in an area closer to her doctors and shopping areas and where she could use the services of Volunteer Wheels. Although Ellen is frightened by her diminishing eyesight, she is grateful for the opportunity to work with a counselor who is helping her to cope with the situation. She is learning how to get around the city by bus; she plans excursions on which her counselor accompanies her to encourage her and to ensure that she arrives home safely. Ellen is learning Braille which she finds fascinating; it reminds her of her younger years when she taught herself shorthand and typing.

Because of her failing eyesight, Ellen has recently given up her job with the Volunteer Center where she sent "thank you" notes and handled other correspondence. She was happy using her skills and is sorry she cannot continue.

Ellen is being challenged in a most difficult way

to know herself and she is meeting that challenge. She is determined that she will not become a prisoner in her home; she wants to make a contribution to others. She is selective about the television programs she allows into her home; she is grateful for "talking books"; and she enjoys meeting people with whom she can share ideas.

Ellen freely admits that she is eighty-five and declares, "I am so irritated about American society's emphasis on youth. As soon as you are over twenty-five you had just as well die, and if you are not beautiful, you really have nothing to live for." Ellen has much to live for. She is still learning to know herself. Although she, like the rest of us, will never completely reach that goal, she is making a sincere effort. Every day she learns more about that person who lives under her skin and inside her head. Socrates would be proud of her.

Y = You

Who are YOU? Who am I? Learning to know YOU, or ME is probably life's toughest lesson. No matter how hard we try we will never know ourselves completely. It is possible, however, to understand ourselves better; that requires courage and determination. It is something only we can do. Others can help, but it is finally up to us. The answers to who we are are within us.

What does it mean to know myself? To "know" anything means "to perceive directly; to recognize; to discern the character." When I know myself, I recognize my strengths and my weaknesses, my positive as well as my negative traits. I know what gives me pleasure; I know what makes me the unique person I am. I know that I can change characteristics I want to change, or I can accept myself just the way I am.

How do I begin the learning process? I begin with a sincere desire to learn. I acknowledge that there are aspects of myself which I know well and some I do not know. I decide to examine the things I know and like about myself as well as those I do not like. I determine to accept the risks and responsibilities that are part of that learning. An important first step is the ability to be able to discriminate between those expectations which come from inside myself and those which come from outside myself. Have I let others determine who I am instead of listening to my own expectations and becoming the person I want to be?

This is a lesson I must learn for myself and from myself. I may meet a fellow student on the same path; we can share our insights and our discoveries, but I still have to do it myself. I can be open to experiences and opportunities that broaden and expand my perceptions. Books written on this subject can be valuable guides, but only guides.

Learning to know myself does not have a monetary cost, but it is expensive in other ways: in effort; in honesty; in recognizing the things I want to change and accepting those I do not want to change.

How will I benefit from knowing myself? The greatest reward is a healthy self-esteem. I will value myself as an interesting and worthwhile person; others will become aware that I value myself and they, in turn, will value me. I will enjoy my own company and the company of others.

When I know myself, I make my own decisions—

I decide what I want, not what someone else thinks is best for me. When I know myself, I can let go of disappointments or failures in my past and use them as stepping-stones in my present and in my future. When I know myself, I know what I do best and what makes me happy. I know my strengths and my weaknesses without labeling them "good" or "bad," and I am not intimidated by anyone. I know that I am the most important person in my world and that I'm O.K. just the way I am.

Z = Zest

26. *Living Life To The Fullest*

Wilma York is a physical fitness zealot. It is apparent upon meeting Wilma that her investment in physical fitness pays generous dividends—she is trim and agile; she radiates good health, and she bubbles with enthusiasm.

Wilma lives at Aldersley, a Danish retirement home, "A Special Place for Special People." The brick Home was built in 1921; its venerable age gives it an air of stability and established beauty. The flowers blooming in every patio add to its charm.

Many of the residents at Aldersley are Danish;

Wilma, however, is not. She was born in Edinburgh, Scotland, and came to the United States with her parents when she was a child. Her father was born in England and her mother in Scotland. Her young parents came to the United States to "seek their fortune and establish a new life." When Wilma's birth was imminent, her mother returned to her homeland to give birth to her "bonnie Scottish lassie."

Nursing was Wilma's career until she retired in 1976. She received her R.N. at Methodist Hospital School of Nursing in Brooklyn, New York, her B.S. at UCLA, and her Masters at University of California School of Nursing Medical School in San Francisco. As an Army Nurse during World War II, from 1943 to 1946, she was Chief Nurse of a 1000-bed Army General Hospital in Liegge, Belgium.

Although Wilma has spent most of her years, since 1936, in California, her adventurous spirit and curiosity have led her to many places. A map of the United States, using a different color for each state where Wilma has lived, would resemble a crazy quilt. At one time she had not seen the Midwest and remedied that by visiting a friend in Minnesota. That visit resulted in two years of teaching at Mankato State University Department of Nursing. She had never been in the South, so she visited a friend in Florida and stayed for several years.

Wilma was on the first Nursing Department faculty at the University of Nevada in Reno where she worked for five years. For ten years she was Director of Public Health Nursing in Marin County, California. One of Wilma's fondest memories is setting up a team-nursing program at a Northern California hospital. Of all the places Wilma lived she chose Marin County as the place to retire.

Wilma enjoys remembering the many and varied places she has been and the experiences she has had, but she doesn't "go back very much . . . I prefer the future; there's so much ahead I want to see and do."

Retirement for Wilma is not a time to sit idly and watch the world go by. In 1980 she wrote a book on physical fitness for older adults; it was designed as a Continuing Education Course of Study for R.N.s, Licensed Vocational Nurses and Nurses' Aides. She co-authored "Fitness for Life," a production of the American Association for Retired Persons (AARP).

Wilma is as active today as she has ever been. Creative Exercise for Seniors is her specialty; this has brought her into all kinds of interesting situations. She appeared as the Exercise Expert on several episodes of the *Over Easy* television program with Mary Martin and Jim Hartz. *Over Easy* was "a nationwide program that explores the personal changes we face in mid-life and beyond." Wilma enjoyed being part of the world of television.

At the same time she was appearing with celebrities on television, Wilma was teaching Creative Exercise for Seniors at Elderhostel at Dominican College in San Rafael, California.

Today, besides attending classes, Wilma teaches health/fitness classes twice a week at the retirement home where she lives. For the past fourteen years she has practiced what she preached by teaching that "you exercise for fun and a future." She teaches dynamic physical fitness to both active and handicapped adults. Her groups have included the visually impaired, senior adult day care centers, convalescent hospitals, and active older adult programs. You will always find clowning and laughing in Wilma's classes— "I like the laughter side of life; sadness distresses me." She learned from her Scotch ancestors their word for sadness which is "dourness." In Wilma's opinion, "If it ain't fun, it ain't worth doing."

Wilma "just happens to fall into" some of her activities. She was attending an all-day seminar at her church and realized that a stretching time was needed in the middle of the morning program and again in the afternoon. She initiated such a program and "Stretch Time" has become a welcome addition to the seminar sessions. The music Wilma uses in her classes and with her "Stretch Time" is important to her; she carefully selects and tapes the music herself to assure that it will be part of the body movement.

Recently Wilma was "having a terrible time. I have all the material for a book on Health and Fitness for Seniors, but I don't know word processing." Wilma is correcting that situation by taking a word-processing class at the college where she has been a student and a teacher.

Wilma's talents and interests are endless and varied. Sometime in her busy life she learned to play her electric organ, and she crochets, recently completing a beautiful afghan in a rose design. She quilts beautifully designed pillow tops and tends her colorful patio garden. Four wall racks display her thimble collection, most of which were gifts from her traveling friends.

For the past four years, Wilma has participated in the 10K Human Race, an annual fund raiser for philanthropic organizations. She recruits and organizes participants from Aldersley and walks the 10K herself. The fact that Wilma is eighty-three does not stop her from doing whatever she decides to do. She is blessed, also, with a special ability to inspire others to live life to the fullest. If it's fun, Wilma wants to be part of it, and she is determined that others will become healthy while they are exercising and enjoying it.

Z = Zest

Zest is the fuel that makes our lives run smoothly. When we keep our tanks filled with zest, we know we will always get where we want to go. Apathy is the sludge that gets in the way and slows us down.

The word that best describes "zest" for me is "enthusiasm." We all know the importance of enthusiasm. The sludge that gets in the way of enthusiasm is boredom. When apathy and boredom have taken over our lives, it is time for a tune-up. How can we get a "life tune-up"? There are many ways:

✓ Find a purpose.

✓ Act as if we are enthusiastic and soon we will be.

✓ Wake up every morning declaring this will be a good day, no matter what it holds.

✓ Do something in a new way—walk a new path, eat our dessert first.

✓ Take a risk, no matter how small.

✓ Listen to someone as we have never listened before—with our hearts as well as our ears.

✓ Find something to laugh about—be sure it is not at someone else's expense.

✓ Relax, relax, relax.

✓ Enjoy, enjoy, enjoy.

There are many excellent tune-up manuals for aging. Among my favorites are:

Going Like Sixty, by Richard Armour

The Courage to Grow Old, edited by Phillip L. Berman

Dr. Burns' Prescription for Happiness, by George Burns

Add Life to Your Years, by Dr. Frank S. Caprio

14,000 Things to Be Happy About, by Barbara Ann Kipfer

Growing Older Getting Better, by Jane Porcino, Ph.D.

Begin to Live, How to Grow Younger as You Get Older, by Dr. Helen Rose

Enjoy Old Age, by B. F. Skinner and M. E. Vaughan

If you find that your life is running on one cylinder, read a tune-up manual, clean out all of the apathy and boredom, fill up with zest and enthusiasm and go merrily on your way. Choose zest, not apathy—enthusiasm, not boredom. You will be surprised how your life purrs along.

Lessons I Have Learned From My A To Z Friends

My friends whose life stories I have had the privilege of writing, have taught me how I can make my own aging a positive experience. They reminded me that old age, no different than babyhood, childhood and adulthood, is a natural segment of the life cycle. Just as becoming a teenager or reaching a 50th birthday is a normal and vital part of life, so is becoming 60, 70, 80 and more.

They have reaffirmed for me that every person is a unique individual and that the older we get, the more "individual" we become. There is no file labeled "old people" in which a person is filed alphabetically or chronologically—we each have our own file and no file contains the same life experiences as that of another.

As I listened to and wrote the life stories, I looked for characteristics, personality traits, circumstances, forces, and early experiences which shaped each life. What determined that person's attitude toward aging? How were the twenty-six lives similar? How were they different?

One experience common to people of my generation is living through the years of the Great Depression. That experience instilled in us an appreciation for simple comforts and a passion for financial security. Another common experience has been our country's involvement in wars; every life has been touched directly or indirectly by war. Many served in the armed forces overseas while others served on the home front.

I found curiosity and a concern for others to be an attribute of people who age positively. I am convinced it is not possible for anyone aging successfully to be selfishly concerned only for himself. And concern for another leads to curiosity about that person, why he thinks and acts as he does, why he is the person he is. Concern leads to acceptance of the other just as he is.

A common thread in some of the stories is an unwavering faith in God. Those individuals give their faith credit for the strength and guidance to work through difficult situations that are a natural and inevitable part of living.

Every person I interviewed has a purpose, something to get up for each day. Each continues to seek opportunities to make choices, to participate in a community, and to be loved and respected. Each has developed his own personal philosophy.

How are we different? In many ways—in personality, appearance, interests, family makeup, health, and in our social lives. Our differences define our individuality.

My friends have taught me:

- that older people, no different than young people, need love, understanding, and a sense of worth;

- that people of all ages need to share, to listen, to be listened to, and to lend a helping hand;

- that more and more older people are healthy, vigorous men and women who lead enjoyable, active lives;

- that life satisfaction depends mainly on how much time we spend doing things we find meaningful;

- that a regular regime of physical activity, mental stimulation, proper nutrition, and well-deserved rest is important to our well-being;

- that we are happier if we don't take ourselves too seriously, if we learn to laugh at ourselves.

Finally, they taught me to be proud of my age, never to be ashamed of it, to wear it as a badge of achievement. My wise friends have inspired me to live my older years so that I can count them among my best years.

INVITATION

I *am inviting you to share a story of positive aging with me. It may be your story or the story of someone you know.*

I *have been inspired by the people whose lives I have shared in this book and I am planning to write another. Your story may be included.*

If you have gained valuable information and inspiration from this book, please let me know.

Best wishes for the best years of your life.

Kay Drikey

Vision Books International
3360 Coffey Lane
Santa Rosa, California 95403